Liane Lefaivre
Döll

CITY

Ground-up
City

Play as a
design tool

PLAY

010 Publishers, Rotterdam 2007

Contents

Applied theory meets reflective practice

a conversation

Henk Döll: Well, then, how did this collaboration get started?
Liane Lefaivre: I must admit, I believed that I had discovered a valuable design tool: the PIP Principle! Almost by chance, of course, in the process of curating the exhibition on Amsterdam playgrounds at the Stedelijk Museum in the summer of 2002. The 40s, 50s and 60s constitute a golden period of urbanism that can still serve as a toolbox today. The post-war approaches differed from the pre-war CIAM approach, which had been excessively, oppressively top-down. In contrast, they were bottom-up or ground-up practices – I like to call them 'dirty real' – that were concerned with the quality of life on the ground, at street level.

As mentioned, the 40s, 50s and 60s represent a period that has tended to be glossed over since post-modernism took over towards the middle of the 1970s. It was generally known that Aldo van Eyck had been involved in the design of playgrounds for Amsterdam during this period, but no one had really looked into the material. Just before he died, I spoke to Aldo and told him I was deeply interested in the playgrounds and in the fact that he had been one of the few major architects to take children as a serious factor in architecture and urbanism throughout his career. It was then that he told me about the existence of an archive about the playgrounds. He died before I managed to locate the archive, which no one had examined in 40 years. I remember Erik Schmitz, the only archivist at the Municipal Archives in Amsterdam who had any idea where to find it. When I finally located him, after having spoken to a dozen other people at the Archives, and the archive Aldo had mentioned, it became clear to me that this was a real treasure house. I got in touch with Rudy Fuchs, the director of the Amsterdam Stedelijk Museum, and asked him if he might be interested in hosting an exhibition on the material. He said Yes, perhaps partly because he had played in one of the playgrounds himself as a child after the war. We only had six months to do the research and to organize the show with the in-house curators.

The show was great popular success both in Amsterdam and internationally. But, as I said, I felt that I had almost accidentally discovered something very relevant to the contemporary situation in the Netherlands, and Europe in general, with regard to multiculturalism and the more general shift in politics towards anti-immigration activities. The debate on the whole question of integration was being carried out in terms which I found very disturbing. I felt that playgrounds could play a constructive role in this situation. I felt not only that children needed to be taken seriously again in urbanism, but that the potential of playgrounds as the locus of a truly public, neighbourhood-generating place in the city-to-be was huge. In the 1960s, Herbert Gans wrote a splendid book called *The Urban Villagers*, about the Italian community in West Boston. It had been a hugely popular book when I was growing up in the 1960s and 1970s. I felt that the key to enhancing the quality of community in inner-city neighbourhoods, in creating an involving sense of urban village, was by updating this historical example of the Amsterdam playgrounds. I wanted to see if it could be applied specifically to multi-cultural neighbourhoods in a city like Rotterdam, with a tough city image. I wasn't so much interested in infusing a spirit of playfulness *per se* in such neighbourhoods, but rather in creating a dispersed, distributed, polycentric public space, bringing people together and opening up the neighbourhood to the outside. I thought that in a network of children's play-grounds would create points of least resistance, I thought of the playgrounds as the smallest stitch in the urban fabric, one that would ensure its cohesion. This tendency to see theory as something to be applied was a natural instinct. I had been attached to Alex Tzonis's group at the TU Delft since its in-cipience. The Design Knowledge Systems Group was prominent throughout the 1980s and 1990s due to its applied approach to research, with its emphasis on the importance of theory not for theory's sake, but for the pro-vision of design tools. In this, we really had to weather the storm of 'pure' post-modern, narcissistic thinking that involved a flight from reality whilst dominating the TU Delft and the Ivy League architecture schools in general.

And just when I was about to give up on the idea of applying this idea of playgrounds to the real world and real people, I received your brochure in the mail announcing that you had opened a new office in Rotterdam. On an impulse, I called you to see if you were interested in testing the PIP tool in the city. It was a highly unusual proposal. Generally theoreticians stay in their ivory towers and practitioners stay in

their offices. This is the only case I know of where a theoretician and a practising office have collaborated in this way. It's amazing when you think of it, actually. I did it because I was discontented with armchair theorizing. What made you agree to it?

It was a coincidence. In 2003 I had just opened a new office and we were establishing a new identity, a little different from Mecanoo, which we had founded some 20 years earlier, in the early eighties. At that time we were still students at the TU Delft, where Aldo van Eyck had been a huge presence, of course. With the new office, we wanted to be engaged in a real city. In Rotterdam we explored the city through our experimental research project 'Lost in Space', in which we studied the social value of public space in this city in 2004. Another important theme was 'Dialogue and Collaboration': we wanted to expand the scope of our practice, to give a more important role to exchange with other professionals and researchers in the field, not only in history, but also in the arts and in other design disciplines.

Prior to that I had been writing about Donald Schön's concept of Reflective Practice, that is, of professional practice always ready to step back and reflect on itself and adapt to new ideas and realities rather than getting stuck in routines. I had already implemented these ideas in my daily work, in the dialogue with clients and future users and in the organizational settings of the practice. But now I would be able to make another step in

the interaction of research and practice, and in the position of the profession in the society at large.

Yes, I remember discussing with you at the time that this was a case of Applied Theory meets Reflective Practice. What I had in mind all along was to have a design tool tested in the field by real practitioners.

Exactly. What I found challenging was that there was nothing dogmatic about this, that it was going to be carried out in a spirit of enquiry. Although I want the practice to uphold a standard of formal design, I also want to make the practice more socially engaged. I may be an exception among architects, but the fact is: I enjoy collaborating. I find it enriching. Probably it's just a question of personality. But I also feel strongly that archi-tectural practice badly needs to expand its agenda. I am becoming increasingly convinced about this and we have now various (inter-national) collaborations with other parties, both within and beyond our own field of work. I think collaborative design in this sense is a not only a very practical approach to problem-solving, but also a necessity for socially engaged international practice.

It's a pity that architects don't take more of a lead in this sense. Architects have a major role to play in creating spatial solutions to social issues, but architectural education doesn't really prepare graduates for dealing with these. And other fields, like sociology for example, suffer from their distance from real design thinking. I think we are beginning to bridge this gap through this project. It actually

24

brings together a variety of topical issues. The image of the city is not doing too well. The most pressing political city debates revolve around how to create a more liveable urban environment with a stronger sense of community among people from different cultural backgrounds. Also the perception of the city as being unsuitable for children is a matter of concern because it drives the middle-income class (families) away. Within this framework, playgrounds can really help. With play for all ages as a highly positive and accessible programme, they may be the only public spaces where people from different backgrounds actually meet and engage in informal contacts.

When Liane put forward this idea of collaborating on play, I realized that playgrounds are never really taken seriously in urban projects. In the end, they are always there, but – unlike themes such as density, street profiles, car parking debates, and other more functional aspects – it's never really an issue. Children and play are simply hardly ever mentioned. The result is that playgrounds are often poorly designed and obligatory. It's a field that has been neglected by architects.

Playgrounds have a specific strength in connecting people to places. This social connection gives identity to public space. It strikes me that playgrounds are often anonymous places with universal play furniture situated in residual or hidden locations. With this project, we are attempting to change this attitude and put playgrounds high on the agenda as a design task again.

The reason I welcomed the idea of updating the Amsterdam playgrounds by 50 years, in a social group much more diverse than that of post-war Amsterdam, is that there are deep similarities in both situations, despite all the changes that have occurred. I thought that this was a real, practical tool for creating public space. Everyone agrees public space is a good thing, although it's also a rather vague concept. The reason things don't always work out in reality, however, is that the rules of the game aren't always clear to people. A lot of lip service is paid, but more often than not plans don't materialize. The appealing thing about the Amsterdam playgrounds in relation to a real inner-city neighbourhood is that they had been tremendously successful in creating a sense of community in a city devastated by a war. They had truly formed a people's public space that had been used and loved. That's the reason the exhibition was so popular in Amsterdam. There was practically no one under the age of 50 who hadn't played in one. In addition, these weren't just any old playgrounds. They were a highly original way of dealing with playgrounds on an urban scale and, more importantly perhaps, with the concept of truly public space as a distributed, polycentric network. There are playgrounds in all cities. But what made the Amsterdam ones unique was the way the city authorities dealt with them in urban terms. That's what I found fascinating about them, and what I tried to define in the PIP model as 'polycentric', 'interstitial' and 'participatory'. I just want to stress how original this approach to

playgrounds is. All these things are clear, I hope, in my contribution to this book.

I thought that it would be good to put the theme of playing in the city on the public agenda once again and use the concept of Amsterdam playgrounds as an inspiring reference. But the next issue was: how to translate these ideas 50 years later into the social and physical context of today. We decided to select two case study areas in Rotterdam. This was in the time that the debate on the multicultural society was raging here. People started realizing that nowadays the majority of inhabitants in some neighbourhoods are of foreign origin and that this is a tendency will spread over the entire city. The social consequences were mainly attacked by divisive strategies. It's obvious that more and more political issues are being defined in a negative sense. Undeniably, there is collective discomfort in the Netherlands and in the Western world in general. But these are mostly dealt with in ways that are defensive. Today, politicians only score when they oppose something and dismiss ideas, not when they are inspiring and creative. To us, the idea of playgrounds, on the other hand, was a more positive way of dealing with these issues.

So, what I wanted to do with this research was to show something else, to show that you can make a positive contribution to social architecture, to a community. It seemed to me that the whole enterprise was worth a try, specifically in Rotterdam. Rotterdam is considered a city that is not child-friendly. In the

25

post-war planning, the layout of the city basically followed the water channels, the railroad tracks, and roads. The infrastructure is dominant. You would expect there would be more interest in space for children in the urban fabric, especially when you consider that a lot of people have children.

To research the applicability of the PIP model as a design tool, we decided to use two very different urban areas as testing grounds. The first one we looked at was Oude Westen, a 19th-century inner-city area with a high-density urban fabric. The multicultural neighbourhood is characterized by an accumulation of problems, such as a high crime rate and many low-income families. It is also the city centre area that accommodates the most children. The other area we selected was Hoogvliet, a typical Dutch post-war neighbourhood designed by Lotte Stam-Beese, which is also a multicultural neighbourhood with a lot of social problems but is located on the outer fringe of Rotterdam. Like many other post-war areas in the Netherlands, Hoogvliet is currently undergoing strong revitalization.

In a way, this was similar to the situation in post-war Amsterdam. The idea of a polycentric, interstitial, participatory network of playgrounds first sprung up in the traditional historical fabric of Amsterdam's centre, and then the idea was transplanted to a very different, post-war new town urban fabric in West Amsterdam by Cor van Eesteren. The transfer of an urban design idea from a traditional fabric to a post-war new town was novel. And it worked.

What we really like about the PIP model is its accent on partici-

pation with real people. The most rewarding part of the process has definitely been the involvement of people and children in the neighbourhoods. With the help of the local institutions, we were able to organize participative sessions with the children to find out what their play culture looks like. The results have inspired us to come up with ideas for a substantiation of a play network linked to specific localities. As a new layer in the urban fabric the network of playgrounds thus truly gives identity to public space.

Now the question remains as to what the next step will be, whether this study will be translated into policy and practice. Our research and the design strategies have already received much attention in the field of public space and play. We are now being invited to appear as keynote speakers and to participate in exhibitions worldwide. But, as we are practitioners, we are also interested in putting our ideas into practice, in testing them, and in advancing the PIP model. We are also extending our ideas: in the multidisciplinary 'playing field' project (*Het Speelveld*) we integrate play and sport in a single concept.

As I said earlier, you should critically reflect on your work through a continuous process of interaction between research and practice. We have experienced that current Dutch policy is not as dynamic and rapid as 50 years ago, when Cornelis van Eesteren and Jacoba Mulder simply commissioned Aldo van Eyck every time they were urged by inhabitants to lay out a playground. Although we are now talking about a few current playground design projects in

Holland, it seems that the first implementation of the PIP principle will be in the deprived neighbourhood of Villa Tranquilla in Buenos Aires, for whose funding which we have just established the PlaySpace Foundation.

I also think this approach to public space can be applied to Europe as a whole. Much of the blame for the riots in the suburbs in Paris can be assigned to architects and town planners, and is related to the simply atrocious architectural conditions people are forced to live in. Many of the social problems at the root of the riots could be solved with the creation of this kind of child-oriented public space in the terms put forth in post-war Amsterdam. I think the idea is worth testing even on a more global scale. I hope that the Villa Tranquilla project in Buenos Aires, which was initiated by Jurgen Rosemann of Delft University of Technology, architect Flavio Janches and myself, is just one instance where the concept for a network of play can be useful. It comes very close to attempts to shape in an 'informal', ground-up manner the public domain all over world, as in the projects designed by Urbanus in Shenzhen, China, Rahul Mehrotra in Mumbai, India, and Teddy Cruz in San Diego and Tijuana, for example. We are, in a way, filling the role of an activist, agit-prop, advocacy NGO, hoping to initiate an improvement in urban life in a ground-up fashion. What distinguishes our efforts in Dutch neighbourhoods is that there is some hope that this approach might get the Mayor and local government involved in funding the programmes we have conceived. But just in case, as you say Henk, it's a good thing to get a foundation going.

DÖLL

THE NATURE OF PLAY

Playgrounds offer little playing space. As demarcated areas that are exclusively intended for child's games, they restrict the essence of play as a part of human nature. Expanding regulations have replaced spontaneous discovery by putting the emphasis on – apparent – safety. Instead of stimulating spontaneity and creativity, most playgrounds offer a configuration of prescriptive items that only hinder a child's imagination. There is a need for an inspiring alternative that cultivates the potential of *homo ludens* in an urban context. A small change in a word, from playground to play space, opens the door to a new perspective. Play space represents mental freedom, and leeway to deviate from the rules. Play space also has significance as a physical margin that enables movement between the different components of a construction or a machine. Play space is something that is for all ages and all places.

The city is full of play. We encounter it in the way in which urban residents appropriate public space. Free minds use buildings, artworks, walls and slopes as a climbing circuit or running track, or they convert the city into a golf course. Those who are inquisitive investigate the clandestine side of the city by visiting prohibited spots in the quiet periods of the day. Older people make their mark on public space by tending street-front gardens, whereas the youth use 'tags'. Physical play spaces can be found in desolate grounds on the edges and in the seams of the city structure. Combined with the infrastructure, they form the slack that the urban machine needs in order to function. Depending on the season, they are transformed into temporary play facilities such as urban beaches and ice rinks. Empty spaces become central meeting places, bringing people of various ages and backgrounds together. In this way, public space acquires identity and cultural value. Premises earmarked for demolition are another phenomenon in which the margins of the city find expression. Their temporary character creates scope to deviate from the regulations. They form the decor for experimental art projects and offer passers-by a moment of revelation in their daily routines. Artists and designers have a role in visualizing play spaces in the city. When their mental freedom is encapsulated in playful interventions, an urban context arises that enables a spontaneous sense of surprise and allows scope for the citizen at play.

ZIMMER MIT AUS-BLICK

URBAN AGRI-CULTURE

URBAN ADVENTURE

FREE-RUNNING

Ingo Vetter,
Berlin, 2002
Residents have appropriated an unused strip of land alongside the former Berlin Wall. Various city groups make use of it. During the daytime, parents arrive with children to play there, enjoy a picnic, or visit the children's farm. In the summer, gypsies use the area to set up a barbecue; at nights, it is a meeting place for young people. The strip is maintained by a group of neighbourhood residents. Dressed like a zebra in the children's farm, Ingo Vetter investigated how this 'autarkic park' functions in a city such as Berlin.

Ingo Vetter
Detroit, 2003-2004
Urban agriculture is a growing phenomenon that primarily occurs in the old centres of American cities that are emptying due to the continual migration to the suburbs. Residents appropriate run-down areas of the city and transform them into vegetable and decorative gardens.

Ruben Dario
Rotterdam, 2005
Urban adventure or urban exploration is the discovery of the hidden sides of the city. In his quest for developing or degenerating locations, Ruben Dario records urban society. Far removed from the organized structures in shopping malls and the self-exhibitionist culture of outdoor cafés, he approaches secluded areas as if they are public spaces.

Los Angeles, 2003
Free-running is the active variant of urban adventure. This sport is occasionally referred to as the Art of Moving, Urban Tricking, or Urban Freeflow. To the stunt people, the entire city is a playground in which they have to use stair banisters, rubbish bins, and walls as parts of a self-conceived circuit. The goal of the urban sport is to create a sense of total freedom.

URBAN GOLF

London, 2005
Urban golf is a the city's response to golf. The city is the golf course and the holes have been replaced by targets such as doors, bus stops, rubbish bins, and billboards. There are fewer regulations than in normal golf. For safety reasons a light, 'almost-golf' ball is used. This sport is rapidly gaining in popularity, also in the Netherlands.

ALLOT-MENTS

Rotterdam, 2006
Allotments are primarily intended for leisure time activity, as a contrast to the pressure of the metropolis. They are being used less and less nowadays, for economic reasons. Growing one's own vegetables has become unnecessary. The allotment is a place of refuge for people of all ages and backgrounds who are looking for a tranquil piece of greenery in the lee of the city.

SHOWING OFF

Amsterdam, 2005
Regardless of how small and limited the living area of the city may be, people tend to appropriate a piece of it and organize it according to their own taste. With this colourful creation, the residents assign identity to public space.

ELVIS IS ALIVE!

Tokyo, Japan 2006
Every Sunday afternoon, dozens of Elvis look-alikes take over the parks in Tokyo. They converge to dance to the music of 'The King', to gape at one another, and to be gaped at. If you stare too long, you have to dance with them.

A DOG'S LIFE

ANGLING

WATER FUN

OLD HABITS

Randstad Agility Association, Rotterdam, September 2006
If you have a dog in the city, you can do more than merely walking it in the park. Temporary play areas have been created for the dog and its master in the green niches and residual seams of the city. They can jointly participate in the dexterity circuits with playing equipment, where all kinds of obstacles have to be taken as quickly as possible.

Oude Maas, Rotterdam, 2006
Besides in wild nature, favourite angling locations can also be found in the urban landscape. It is usually men who recurrently visit their preferred spot on a canal or inland waterway. Armed with a rod, stool and cool box, they play their favourite game in deepest concentration.

Fontein Beurstraverse Rotterdam, 2006
To many adults, shopping is a game in itself. In the semi-sunken mall in Rotterdam, the shopping street becomes a veritable playground when all kind of water sprays unexpectedly shoot out of the ground in the summer. Shopping has never been so much fun for children.

Rotterdam, 2006
The sight of young people hanging around in public space often leads to the submission of complaints by local residents. The fact that not only the youth but also the elderly also succumb to the natural tendency to seek one another's company places society in a dilemma.
The Dutch village of Oude Pekela gained national fame when a group of old people were prohibited from gathering together because their zimmers and scootmobiles were an obstacle to the shopping public.

31

URBAN BEACH

Rotterdam, 2006
In an increasing number of large cities, season-related events are being organized on otherwise desolate sites. They are converted to temporary playing and meeting places for young and old. In the summer, city residents sunbathe, sport and drink here on improvised beaches that become instant hot spots.

WINTER PLAZA

Rotterdam, 2005
When nature lets us down when it comes to frost, the city provides a welcome alternative that gives at least as much fun to many. Ice rinks are created at the left-over urban spaces that function as beaches in the summer. You can bring your own ice skates or hire them at the desk. Or you can just sit and watch with a glass of *glühwein* in your hands.

HANAMI MATSURI

Japan
At the beginning of May, all Japanese people go out to admire the flowering sakura (cherry blossom). This age-old tradition is called 'hanami': 'hana' means 'flower' and en 'mi' means 'to look'. 'Matsuri' means 'festivity'. People go picnicking and partying under the sakura trees in the park. The park thus acquires a special significance for urban residents.

STREET FOOT-BALL

Buenos Aires, 2005
Football has returned to where it once begun: on the streets. Street football is an effective way of stimulating sport among young people because this activity harmonizes with their lifestyle. The widest street in the world in Buenos Aires was even specially vacated for the South American Street Football Tournament in 2005.

BLUE HOUSE

Florentijn Hofman, Rotterdam, 2004
The transience of old premises, earmarked for demolition creates scope for surprising approaches. The Municipality relaxes the regulations and allows artists free rein. The city becomes the painter's canvas. In 2004, the artist Florentijn Hofman painted the facade of a building due for demolition in Rotterdam with 700 litres of blue paint. This 'heavenly marking' became a striking phenomenon in public space.

HORMIGAS

Martiriá Figueras, Spain, 2003
Martiriá Figueras changed a boring grassy field adjoining a sewage works into an attractive, distinctive and symbolic exterior space. She created a design for eight gigantic ants made of polyester with iron legs. They are movable and glow in the dark. The sober grounds are now a dynamic playful landscape.

VILLA DEPONIE

Dan Peterman, Italy, 2002
Artist Dan Peterman plays with recycled materials. He is particularly interested in organic processes in urban society. His work is accessible and stimulating. Villa Deponie entices people to look at their surroundings in a different way. Although it is not intended as an object of play, it is often used as such by the general public.

STADT-LOUNGE

Pipilotti Rist and Carlos Martinez, Sankt Gallen, Switzerland, 2005
In the Stadt-lounge, fountains, benches and even a car are covered by a layer of bright-red tartan. The alienation that this design evokes induces all kinds of spontaneous play by users of all ages. In the evening, the entire complex is illuminated.

33

PINK GHOST

BADE-SCHIFF

Périphériques Architectes, Paris, 2002
The design entitled Pink Ghost by Périphériques Architectes transforms a square in Paris into a bright-red living room, complete with fixed tables and chairs. The light-footedness of the design stimulates passers-by who seem to figure as theatre actors in this surrealistic decor.

Susanne Lorenz, Berlin, 2004
The fact that not only space on land can be used in an exceptional way, but also that in the water, is proved by the traditional Berlin Badeschiffe, swimming pools in the river. The artist Susanne Lorenz revitalizes Berlin bathing culture with her modern Badeschiff in the River Spree. This bathing place has a great power of attraction on playful urban residents and tourists.

LIANE LEFAIVRE

GROUND-UP CITY

THE PLACE OF PLAY

Introduction

I use the expression 'ground-up city' in an intentionally equivocal way, in both of its possible senses. In the first, it means broken, fragmented, in a state of disintegration as opposed to cohesive and integrated. In the other, it is a synonym for a bottom-up, community-driven and informal as opposed to top-down and formal.

Whichever way one codes the term, the ground-up city has gotten about as low as it gets on the professional architectural and urban agenda, which is now almost entirely governed by a neo-liberalist, profit-centred mentality which Denise Scott Brown has caustically referred to as 'go-for-the jugular', bent on serving what Richard Florida calls the 'creative class'.[1]
If there is possible contender that is even more abysmal on the profession's set of priorities, that is the subject of playgrounds. The reasons for abandoning them, many of which are legitimate, will be addressed in the present book.

Playgrounds and the ground-up city. The present book is an attempt to lift these notions up from the lower depths to which they have sunk in the opinion of architects and urbanists, and show how beneficial the relation between them can be, particularly in the creation of emergent public space.

The place of play in art

This is not to say that no architect or urbanist is attempting to inject playfulness into cities. There are a few, but they tend to be the exceptions to the rule: Enric Miralles and Benedetta Tagliabue designed the *Rosario Municipal Center* (1997) in Barcelona for example, NL designed the *Basketbar* at the University Campus of Utrecht, the Uithof (2003), and Gary Chang built *Leisure Slice,* a modular, mobile play structure in Hong Kong (2005) to name but three.

More often than not, artists take up the task of creating playful urban designs. They are more actively engaged in the creation of urban play situations than architects and urbanists are. Moreover, many of their works tend to be extremely funny, even hilarious. They also tend to be very high profile. Erwin Wurm's *One Minute Sculptures* and his *Play Sculpture* (2004), Fischli and Weiss's miniature office building in a parking lot (2000), Dan Graham and Jeff Wall's various playgrounds, Vito Acconci's *Klein Bottle Playground* (2000), Pipilotti Rist's and Carlos Martinez's *Urban Living Room* in Bleicheli, St Gallen (2005), Nils Norman's *Adventure Playgrounds* scheme for the Financial District in London[2] and Carsten Höller's *Test Site* (2006) at the Tate Modern are recent cases in point. (Figs.1 a-h)

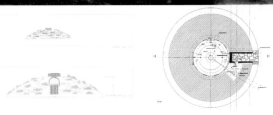

Figs.1a, b, c
Dan Graham and
Jeff Wall, *Children's
Pavilion,* 1989
(courtesy of
Dan Graham).

Playfulness is concept that is central to many major contemporary artists' work in a way that does not apply to architects and urbanists. Dan Graham, for example, claims that the gradual realization, starting in the 1980s, that children were interested in the playful aspect of his work prompted him reorient it, making it even more playful it in order to engage children, pointing out that the Dia Foundation Pavilion (see Appendix 1) was first intended as a playground.

Erwin Wurm is equally explicit about the importance of playfulness in his art, as well as art in general. When asked if he agreed with Huizinga's *Homo Ludens* theory that play is really the basis of civilization, Wurm could not have been more positive: '…that is (the role of) play. Absolutely. Sadness is always presented as having imposing cultural importance and I think it is wrong, it is just wrong. Playfulness should be taken far more seriously'. (See Appendix 2.) For the purposes of this essay, in fact, Wurm even provided me with his designs for the playground that are reproduced here.

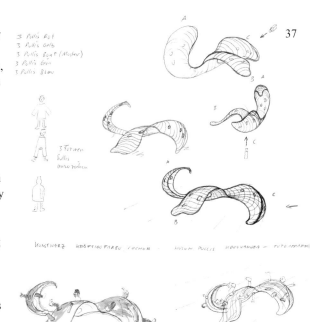

37

Figs.1d, e, f
Erwin Wurm,
*Playground Project
for the MAK,* 2004
(courtesy of
the artist).

1. The use of the term 'neoliberalist' here is based on David Harvey's *A Brief History of Neo-Liberalism*, Oxford, Oxford University Press, 2005. For a criticism of the abandonment of the social commitment of the architectural profession in the mid-70s, see Alexander Tzonis and Liane Lefaivre, 'The Narcissist Phase of Architecture', *Harvard Architecture Review*, I, Spring 1980. pp. 52-61. 'Creative Class' is based on Richard Florida's *The Rise of the Creative Class*, New York, Basic Books, 2002. Denise Scott Brown, 'Urban Design at Fifty, and a Look Ahead', *Harvard Design Magazine*, Spring/Summer 2006, pp. 33-44.
2. Nils Norman, *An Architecture of Play: a Survey of London's Adventure Playgrounds*, London, Four Corners Books, 2003.

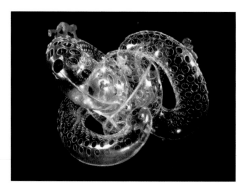

Fig.1g
Carsten Höller,
Test Site, 2006
(courtesy of
the Tate Modern,
London).

38

Fig.1h
Vito Acconci, *Klein
Bottle Playground*,
2000
(courtesy of
Dan Graham).

As for Fischli and Weiss, when I interviewed them, Peter Fischli declared that 'If somebody would come and suggest we should design a playground, I would say Yes.'[3] Jerome Sans (Fig.2), former co-director of the Palais de Tokyo in Paris, was the most categorical of all about the general importance of play in art. To him 'all art is a game'. (Appendix 3.)

According to Freud,[4] funny things cause laughter because they release us from our inhibitions by allowing us to express intentions and thoughts that would otherwise have remained hidden. The stronger the inhibition, the more hilarious our reaction is to sensing it being shattered. In other words, funny things contain a varying potential for subverting the rules, for re-inventing them.

The element of subversion and re-invention is something the works of these artists share with all works of art. But there is another dimension to their antics. This is the Dadaist tradition to which they belong, stretching back to the period immediately following the First World War, when many artists – interestingly no architects – sought out the therapeutic, liberating irrationality of play in the wake of the war's deeply traumatic, dehumanizing events as a means of 'taming the savageness of life' as Friedrich Schiller might have put it.[5] One answer to this dehumanization was an explosion of playfulness in the arts. Duchamp's Dadaist works, like the *Urinal* of 1917 and the mustachioed Mona Lisa of *L.H.O.O.Q.* (1919) were the first of these. Similarly, during the 1920s, Arnold Schoenberg invented magic playing cards, a domino set, and a game called *Coalition Chess*, a version of chess for four players instead of two and whose very nature makes it impossible to win.[6] (Figs.3a,b) Marcel Duchamp gave up all other activities in 1923 and devoted his life to playing chess. The sculptor Alexander Calder, who, as a child, had always designed toys for his sister, created his *Cirque Calder* (1926-30), and Kurt Schwitters put together his ticker-tape *Merzbilder*.[7]

City as a gameboard

This was also when the Surrealists made play their main compositional principle.[8] The *Cadavre Exquis* was a game invented by them around 1925. According to the *Dictionnaire abrégé du surréalisme*, it was a game that consisted of generating a sentence or a drawing by several people without them being able to see the previous contributions. The first example was 'Le cadavre - exquis - boira - le vin - nouveau' invented by Marcel Duhamel, Jacques Prevert, and Yves Tanguy. Andre Breton used this originally purely playful activity, and made it a means of creating poetic imagery. (Médium no.2, 1954). The automatism of this game made it similar to the Surrealist concept of errance, used in order to transform Paris into a giant gameboard, first in Louis Aragon's *Le Paysan de Paris* (1927), then with André Breton's wandering through Paris in *Nadja* (1928), and Man Ray's collection of Atget's photography.[9] In all cases, what occurred was an aimless, automatic, good-natured wandering or flânerie, away from the bourgeois boulevards and squares, and the discovery of another, more mysterious Paris. Like the later Situationist psycho-geographic dérive of the 1950s directly inspired by the errance, such exercises were meant to provide an alternative to the oppression of stiflingly conventional bourgeois urban life, of consumer culture and the world of work, and replace it with a strange, unfamiliar, quirky one that allows one to imagine a possible alternative.

Equally in the tradition of Dadaism were the artists who participated in the first playful urban Happenings, like Allan Kaprow (who first coined the term in the Spring of 1957), George Segal, John Cage, Robert Rauschenberg, Jim Dine, Carolee Schneeman and Merce Cunningham in the late 1950s, setting the tone for the 1960s urban performances such as of Hans Hollein's *Mobile Office (1966),* Coop Himmelblau's *Restless Ball* (1971) and Haus-Rucker-Co's *Balloon for Two (1972)*[10] as well as for urban-scale installations like Claes Oldenburg's *Colossal Monument for 42nd street* in the form of a banana (1965), James Wines's *Best Department Stores* (1970s), Niki de Saint Phalle and Jean Tinguely's *Fontaine de Stravinsky* (1982-1983) (Fig.3c). The same is true of installations in natural settings, such as Hans Hollein's *In-Between Building* (1968) (Fig.3d), Robert Wilson's first design project, *Poles, a playground for Loveland, Ohio* (1968), consisting of gigantic poles lined up in order to teach children how to count through the dynamics of movement (Fig.4),[11] and Jean Dubuffet's gigantic sculptures such as the *Closerie Falbala* (1971-73) and his *Jardin d'email* (1974).

Fig.2
'Curator Imperator': 'fat' portrait of Jerome Sans by Erwin Wurm, 2003 (courtesy of the artist).

39

Fig.3a,b
Arnold Schönberg, *Coalition Chess*, approx. 1920, Chessmen in the form of WWI military personnel and arms, and set-up areas and starting position (by permission of Balmont Music publishers).

3. Interview of Peter Fischli and David Weiss by Liane Lefaivre, 23 November 2004, Zurich. They allowed me to tape the interview but not to publish it.
4. Sigmund Freud, *Jokes and their Relation to the Unconscious.*
5. Friedrich Schiller, *The Aesthetic Letters*, Boston, Little Brown, 1920. Letter 15.
6. Ernst Strouhal, 'Es musste moglich sein...Arnold Schoenberg – Konstruktionen, Modelle, Spieledesigns', *Arnold Schoenberg, Games, Constructions Bricolages*, Vienna, Arnold Schoenberg Center, 2004. See also Allen Shawn, *Arnold Schoenberg Journey*, New York, Farrar, Strauss, 2006.
7. See Jacob Baal-Teshuva and Alexander Calder, *Calder: 1898-1876*, Cologne, Taschen, 1998.
8. *Faites vos Jeux. Kunst und Spiel seit Dada*. Austellungs Katalog, Viaduz, 2005.
9. Louis Aragon, Le Paysan de Paris, 1926; Andre Breton, *Nadja*, 1928; Susan Laxton, *Paris as a Gameboard. Man Ray's Atget*, New York, Wallach Art Gallery, 2002.
10. The best overview of the Viennese school is to be found in Dominique Rouillard, *Superarchitecture. Le Futur de l'architecture 1950-70*. Paris, Villette, 2005.
11. See Amanda Otto-Bernstein, *Absolute Wilson*, Munich, Prestel Verlag, 2006, and the movie of the same name, 2006.

Fig.3c
Niki de Saint Phalle
and Jean Tinguely,
*Fontaine à
Stravinski*, Paris,
1981, photographed
by Alberto Bezzola
(courtesy of Alberto
Bezzola).

40

Taming the Savageness of Life

The idea that play is important precedes the Dadaist movement, of course. Friedrich Schiller (1759-1805), who abandoned a military career and high rank to become a playwright, poet and philosopher, wrote, in the 15th of his *Aesthetic Letters* of 1793, that 'man only plays when he is a man in the full meaning of the word, and he is only completely a man when he plays', and 'man is never so serious as when he plays'. With these words, he became the first notable writer in Western culture not only to extol the value of play in general terms, but to see it as the very essence of human nature thus countering the Kantian cult of reason as put forth more specifically his Critique of Judgment, and opening the way to romanticism. His justification for this was far from frivolous. For him, play was, to recall the previous quote above, a way to 'tame the savageness of life'.[12]

The Swiss psychologist Karl Groos (1861-1946), writing over a hundred years after Schiller, was the second. In *The Play of Animals* (1896), he assigned play an important genetic role in the growth of intelligence in animals and humans. He first studied play behaviour in animals. The kitten playing with the ball of yarn, he noted, is preparing to be the cat teasing the mouse. The dog playing at fighting and biting is exercising himself to be the victor in encounters in which dogs really fight and bite. This extends throughout all the playful activities of an animal species. Curiously, but reasonably within this theory, they show bungling and tentative imitations of the adult habits of the species. 'Instead of saying animals play because they are young, we must say that animals have youth in order that they may play.' Play, in other words, may have – and probably did have, he believed – a role in the formation of animal adult intelligence.[13] Generalizing from animal to human psychology in *The Play of Humans* (1899), he wrote that 'play leads from what is easy to more difficult tasks, since only deliberate conquest can produce the feeling of pleasure in success', and that play plays an important role in human the development of intelligence in general.[14]

This view influenced an important paper by Sigmund Freud, who saw play as central in human nature. His works on the topic of play included *Jokes and their Relation to the Unconscious*, and *Beyond the Pleasure Principle*. In his *The Role of Play and Daydreaming in the Poetic Imagination*, written in 1908,[15] he argued that childhood play is the source of creative thinking in the adult. Just as the child learns through play to re-arrange features of the real world, the creative person does the same, he believed. '... A piece of creative writing, like a day-dream, is a continuation of, and a substitute for, what was once the play of childhood,' he wrote.

If the theme of play appears in one paper of Freud's, it is practically everywhere in the writings of Jean Piaget. More than any other writer he viewed childhood play as a key element in human cognition and the growth of intelligence. One of his earliest books, *Play, Dreams and Imitation in Childhood*, first published in 1936, put forth most forcefully the role of play, which he saw as an attempt to imitate the behaviour of adults and adapt to grown-up society, as the basic way a child acquires new knowledge and constructs reality. This point of view will be a mainstay of his subsequent writings, and will inform his other writings. In fact he is responsible for the 'learning by play' approach to education, which he found more effective than rote learning.[16]

No one has ever valued play more than Johann Huizinga. His *Homo Ludens* was written in 1938. It argues that play is not only the essence of human nature, as Schiller had written, but also of human culture and civilization. In his words, '… It was not my object to define the place of play among other manifestations of culture, but rather to ascertain how far culture itself bears the character of play.' Play assumes a particular meaning for him. He saw it as a set of rules whose principle role was to ritualize and therefore undermine and subvert the aggressive spirit of competition and contest by submitting it to rules, so that play had a civilizing function. To him, religion, language, law, art, and sport were all systems of rules for containing aggression, or, to go back to Schiller's expression, to 'tame the savageness of life'.

However, Huizinga was not the first to champion this function. The people in charge of Dutch cities four hundred years ago also took a similar approach. Judging from the evidence put forth in Simon Schama's *The Embarrassment of Riches*, Huizinga's theory of the civilizing role of children's play had deep roots in Dutch culture, particularly urban culture. As Schama pointed out, kinderspelen or 'children's play', represented in readily recognizable urban settings, formed a topic of Dutch painting and Northern humanist culture in general that went back to at least the sixteenth century. He makes the point that the ubiquity of children in Dutch painting, not as allegorized *putti* or the 'immortal child' but as real beings, is another side of the same tradition. 'Nothing

Fig.3d
Hans Hollein, *Fit-in Building*, 1968 (courtesy of Atelier Hollein).

Fig.4
Robert Wilson, *Poles,* 1967, photographed 1968, photographer unknown (courtesy of Byrd Hoffman Water Mill Foundation).

12. Friedrich Schiller, *The Aesthetic Letters*, Boston, Little Brown, 1920. Letter 15.
13. Karl Groos, *Die Spiele der Tiere*, 1896. English translation: *The Play of Animals*, tr. E.L. Baldwin, N.Y., Appleton, 1898.
14. Karl Groos, *Die Spiele der Menschen,* 1899. English translation: *The Play of Man*. Tr. E.L. Baldwin, New York, Appleton, 1901.
15. Sigmund Freud, 'Creative Writers and Daydreaming', *Complete Works of Sigmund Freud*, trans. J. Strachey, 9: 141-153. London, 1965.
16. Jean Piaget, *Play, Dreams and Imitation in Childhood*, NY, Norton 1990, first published in French, 1936. He elaborated on the same theory of play in T*he Origins of Intelligence in Children*, New York, Norton, 1963 (first pub. 1936) and *The Construction of the Real in Childhood*, New York, Norton, 1990, (first published 1937).
17. Simon Schama, *The Embarrassment of Riches* (New York: Collins, 1987), p. 495.

illustrates the peculiar bias of the Dutch culture towards children and the world than the compendia they put into paint, print, and even wall tiles. There was a *kinderspelen* series of pictures, embodying the conflicts between diversion and instruction, between freedom and obedience, between exploration and safety. By situating the games not in the 'imaginary vacuum of time and space' but in topographically meaningful settings – nearly always with some public building, a town hall or guildhall – they evoke the civic and public virtues to which the child should be led. 'When we see them,' Schama writes, 'we are more not merely glimpsing snapshots from a family album, but scenes from the interior of the Dutch mental world.'

As Schama again points out, what is striking about the humanist – in the deepest sense of the term – *kinderspelen* tradition, which was probably the origin of the urban playground that spread around the world in the next three centuries, is 'the absence of any other than children in these public places'. This tradition in painting, unique to Dutch culture, had a foundation in reality. It was not so much an expression of *homo ludens* for the sake of play alone. Nothing much in Dutch culture is ever far from some form of pragmatism. As in the case of Huizinga's theory of play, playgrounds in Dutch cities filled a practical purpose, according to Schama. They reflected the wish to instill republican values, a republican sense of community, in children from an early age, and to bring them into the fold of the reality of civic life in a bourgeois society. The most efficient way to set up this learning process with young children, of course, was in a play setting.[17]

Magnet City, Tinkertoy Architecture

Of course, the *kinderspelen* paintings were just a subset of a more general if, again, unique genre in Dutch painting representing the city as a playground for adults. Well-known artists depicting such scenes included Jan van Goyen, Adam van Breem, Christoffel van den Berghe, Adriaen van de Venne, Henrick Avercamp, Hans Bol, Jan Beerstratten, Jacob Grimmer, David Vingboons, not to mention Pieter Bruegel the Elder (Fig.5).[18] It is interesting to speculate that the Dutch cities might have been the first to have introduced play as a part of everyday life, as opposed to restricting it to specially institutionalized carnival periods. Certainly, there is a long unbroken tradition of urban play furniture (Figs.6, 7).

The most notable architect of the twentieth century to allow the imperative of playfulness take over in his designs is, no doubt, Cedric Price. The idea for the *Fun Palace* (1959-61), never built, was supposedly first concocted by Price and the theatre director Joan Littlewood when walking on 42nd Street on a visit the

Fig.5
Hendrick Avercamp (1585-1634), *Winter Landscape with Ice Skaters*, undated (by permission of Rijks Museum, Amsterdam).

Fig.6
Pieter Brueghel the Elder (1525/30-1569), *Children's Games*, 1560, detail (by permission of Kunsthistorisches Museum, Vienna).

Fig.7
One of Aldo van Eyck's Playgrounds, 1950s (courtesy of Municipal Archives, Amsterdam).

two made to America. The design reflected the increasing whimsy of post-imperial Britain. A Fun Palace? This was a clear departure from the dullness, conformity and sterility associated with Britain's technocratic welfare state. Price and Littlewood intended the building to be a colossal, Dadaist playground for adults. As with the Dutch playground, the purpose of the Fun Palace was half-didactic and half-playful. Intended to be housed within an immense steel and glass-structure, with cranes permanently affixed to the walls thus enabling walls and floors to be constantly rearranged like Tinkertoys,[19] the Fun Palace was conceived as an interactive, performative, universal space accommodating a great variety of artistic events. It produced a new kind of improvisational architecture to negotiate the constantly shifting cultural activities. It was not a building in any conventional sense, but was instead a built piece of agit-prop, highly adaptable to the constantly changing conditions. Littlewood had conceived a new kind of theatre, designed to awaken the passive subjects of mass culture to a new con-sciousness. Her vision of a dynamic and interactive theatre provided the programmatic framework on which Price would develop and refine this concept. By assembling their own pedagogical and leisure environ-ments using cranes and prefabricated modules in an improvisational architecture, common citizens could escape from everyday routine and serial existence and embark on a journey of learning, creativity, and individual fulfilment (Fig.8).

Price hatched the *Potteries Thinkbelt* scheme in 1964, an iconoclastic proposal for a university housed in mobile train wagons and the abandoned paleo-technic Pottery factories in Staffordshire, linked together along an old rail track. There was always a political element to Price's work, an ebullient fusion of instruction and delight, socialism and surrealism. As he wrote of the *Potteries Thinkbelt*: 'Education, if it is to be a continuous human service run by the community, must be provided with the same lack of peculiarity as the supply of drinking water or free teeth.' His *Nonplan*, produced in 1969 along with the urban planner Sir Peter Hall and sociologist Paul Barker, argued that cities were over-regimented and permitted no element of play. Consistent with his belief in Pop-up Parliament, a project of 1965, Price argued that there was too much legislation and that Parliament should appear only to set limits when absolutely necessary. More recent projects brought these themes to specific urban contexts. His *Magnet City* project (throughout the 1990s) proposed the creation of in-between spaces – steps to the subway,

LEA RIVER SITE

Fig.8
Cedric Price, *Fun Palace*, 1961 (by permission of Canadian Center for Architecture, Montreal / Collection Centre Canadian d'Architecture).

43

18. See B. Haak, *The Golden Age. Dutch Painters of the Seventeenth Century*, London, Thames and Hudson, 1984.
19. Herbert Muschamp, 'Cedric Price, Influential British Architect with Sense of Fun, dies at 68', *New York Times ,23 Aug. 2003*.

bus stops, shopping streets – as triggers of urbanity to stimulate new patterns of encounter.[20]

The younger and zanier Archigram group was inspired by Cedric Price's exuberant spirit, as well as by the theorist, critic and fellow eccentric, gizmo-loving Reyner Banham.[21] It became famous for its hare-brained, wild design attacks upon the technocratic design of the welfare state. Its approach to architecture was fun too, like Cedric Price's, as illustrated by two of the group's most memorable projects: Ron Herron's 1964 cartoon drawings of a *Walking City*, in which a city of giant, reptilian structures literally glided across the globe on enormous legs until its inhabitants found a place where they wanted to settle; and the crane-mounted living pods that could be plugged in wherever their inhabitants wished in Peter Cook's 1964 *Plug-in City*. Equally irreverent was the madcap, techno-logically optimistic devices that Archigram dreamt up to fulfill the functions of traditional buildings, from miniaturized capsule homes like Ron Herron and Warren Chalk's 1965 *Gasket Homes* and David Greene's 1966 *Living Pod*, or Michael Webb's 1966 *Cushicle*, a mobile room on wheels, and his 1967 wearable house, the *Suitaloon*. In 1968, the group proposed to transport all the entertainment and education resources of a metropolis in an *Instant City* airship, which would fly from place to place and temporarily 'land' in small communities to enable the inhabitants to enjoy the buzz of life in a city.[22] In 1969, the group opened an architectural practice after winning a competition to design a leisure centre in Monte Carlo. The design was of an enormous circular dome on land reclaimed from the Mediterranean Sea. The seats, toilets and lights were mounted on wheels to be moved around into new configurations as the use of the building changed.

Amsterdam Playgrounds:
Dadaist Playfulness combined with Civil Service

Architects and urbanists have not always had the particularly anti-playful mindset they display nowadays. There have been times when they came up with their share of playfulness in designs of their own, and there have been times when they have come up with inventive, effective designs for public space with the aim of bringing people together – as we shall see further on.

The post-war Amsterdam playgrounds are a rare example of both – an exercise in both Dadaist playfulness and civil service. In 1947 there were fewer than 30 playgrounds in the city. This is the same number as in 1929, when Cornelis van Eesteren, the erstwhile new director of the Municipal Department of

Public Works, commissioned a series of city maps. One map marked the location of the city's public toilets. Another, its open-air markets. Another, its garages. Another, its public telegraph and telephone booths. The fifth indicated the location of the playgrounds of the city.[23]

Even the most superficial glance at these maps of Amsterdam is revealing. Although playgrounds for children was one of Van Eesteren's five main concerns, the presence of children was minor compared with that of urinating adults, adults shopping for food at market stalls, adults taking care of their cars in garages, and adults calling other adults on public telephones (Figs.9,10).

But, by 1968, the situation was radically different. Amsterdam had over 1000 playgrounds. This means no fewer than 50 playgrounds were designed and produced every year from 1947 onward – a gigantic number. They spread from the historical centre of Amsterdam to the new towns to the West of Amsterdam – Sloterdijk, Slotermeer, and Geuzeveld. Each playground was individually dealt with by Van Eesteren and his associate Jacoba Mulder. Each was designed by Aldo van Eyck.

Built up over a period of just over 20 years, the post-war Amsterdam playgrounds were a remarkable success story. Indeed, it can be said that they were the first example not only of a new type of playground design, but also, in general, of a new, post-Second World War approach to public space and urban design.

In order to understand what made the post-war Amsterdam playgrounds such a resounding success at the time – as well as argue, perhaps more controversially, that they are even more useful than ever before in some urban environments today, specifically multicultural inner-city neighbourhoods – it is necessary to look at the 'Big Picture'. This picture has two very different parts: on the one hand, the cultural value of play, and, on the other, the place of play in the world of urban government and governance.

The Rise of Post-war Playgrounds

The idea of play gave rise to a wave of interest in the architectural profession immediately following World War II, this time involving playgrounds for children. It grew out of what might be termed the post-war phenomenon of 'child empowerment'.[24] The post-war baby boom produced another bottom-up effect.

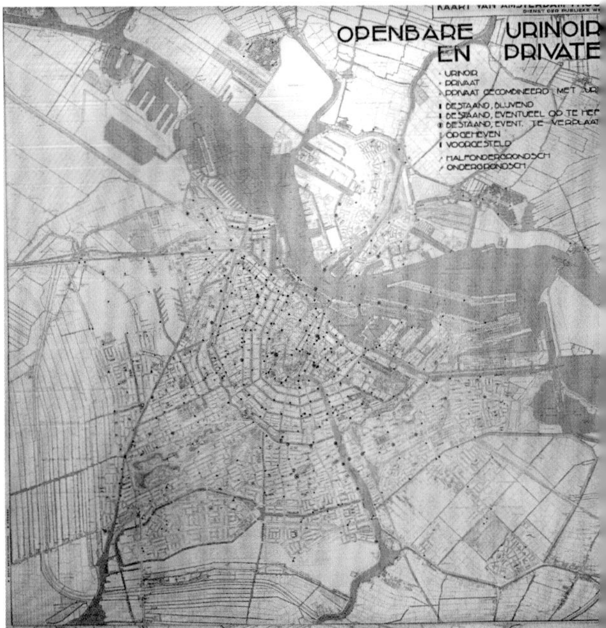

Fig.9
Map of public toilets in Amsterdam, 1929, Public Works Department, Cornelis van Eesteren Archives, NAi, Rotterdam.

Fig.10
Map of the 29 playgrounds of Amsterdam, 1929, Public Works Department, Cornelis van Eesteren Archives, NAi, Rotterdam.

20. Cedric Price, Works II, London, A.A., 1984. Stanley Matthews, From Agit-Prop to Free Space. The Architecture of Cedric Price, London, Black Dog Publishing, 2006; Cedric Price et al, Re: CP, ed. Hans Ulrich Obrist, Basel, Birkhauser, 2003.
21. Reyner Banham
22. Peter Cook, Archigram, London, Studio Vista, 1972.
23. NAi, Archief Van Eesteren, 1.267-284.
24. This point is a reiteration of Liane Lefaivre, 'Space, Place and Play', Aldo van Eyck, the Playgrounds and the City, Amsterdam, Stedelijk Museum, 2003.

Children, the lowest on the social rung and also the weakest, could no longer be simply dictated to. They became empowered as never before in many arenas of life – political, cultural, economic, domestic. In 1948, the United Nations General Assembly adopted a Declaration of the Rights of the Child. This new attitude toward childhood spread rapidly in the social sciences. Perhaps the first sign of change was Benjamin Spock's revolutionary and epoch-making *The Common Sense Book of Baby and Child Care* (1946) that gave more power to the child in the domestic environment.[25] Child psychology became widely accepted in universities, and as a field of psychology in its own right among the general public. Anna Freud, for example, set up the Hampstead Child Therapy Training Courses and Clinic in 1947. Psychologist Erik Erikson wrote *Childhood and Society* in 1950. In the field of consumption, this was a time when Disneyland and its most effective advertising engine, the Mickey Mouse Show, were created, turning the child into a powerful force of consumption. Early evening television was monopolized by children's shows, laced with advertisements to program children to become faithful buyers of special brands of breakfast cereals, sweet bubbly drinks and deserts, while their mothers were encouraged to purchase detergents at the supermarket. In cinema, the theme of childhood becomes the subject of in-depth studies with neo-realist Italian films like Vittorio de Sica's *The Bicycle Thief* (1948) and *Miracolo a Milano* (1950), and in France, the *Nouvelle Vague*'s Jean-Pierre Melville's *Les Enfants Terribles* (1949). While English photographer Nigel Henderson's wife was carrying out sociological studies on children in working class areas of Great Britain, he photographed them. Another famous photographer interested in the post-war urban child was Robert Doisneau in Paris.

Child's art became an object of imitation among the major artists of the immediate post-war period. This is notably true of Jean Dubuffet and Juan Miró. It is well known that Jackson Pollock's paintings were attempts to express primitive, naïve, childlike drives.[26] The COBRA group, too, consisting of Asger Bjorn, Constant, Corneille and Karel Appel among others, began to explicitly imitate child's art in their official magazine (also called COBRA) and devoted the 4th issue of the magazine, which coincided with an exhibition curated by Willem Sandberg at the Stedelijk Museum in Amsterdam in 1949, to the theme of childhood.[27] This is where paintings such as Corneille's *Les Jeux d'Enfants et Le Grand Soleil* (1948) were presented for the first time. The issue reproduced children's drawings and modern primitive naïve painters. In it, Corneille wrote that 'Aesthetics is a tic of civilization. Art has nothing to do with beauty;

imagination is the way to learn the truth.' Constant, for his part, wrote: 'The child knows no other rule but his own spontaneous life feeling, and has no other need but the need to express it.' Why? According to Constant, "It is also this property that lends these cultures such a power of attraction to the people of today who have to live in a morbid atmosphere of falsity, lies, and infertility.'[28] The spontaneous art of children inspired us more than the oeuvre of professional artists.[29] Aldo van Eyck's architectural renderings in children's crayons of some of the playgrounds also share another element with COBRA art. Willem Sander himself, the director of the Stedelijk Museum, organized his first post-war exhibition in 1947 on the theme of Art and the Child at the museum, based on a selection he made of children's paintings that had been organized by the Association Française d'Action Artistique in Paris.[30]

The baby boom had an impact among urban theorists, most particularly among those who were interested in community. In an article published in 1949, Lewis Mumford pleaded for the creation of playscapes in cities.[31] Chicago's *Journal of Housing* of July 1949 also published illustrations of Danish playgrounds. To the American urban theorist Kevin Lynch, the child's perception of urban space is so important that he based much of his research throughout the 1950s on it, and placed a child's drawing on the cover of his famous book, *The Image of the City* (1960).[32] He returned to the theme in a later Unesco-sponsored book on *Growing Up in Cities* (1970).[33] (Fig.11)

Luis Barragàn was a garden designer who became renowned in the field of children's facilities. His 1934 playground design for Parque de la Revolución in Guadalajara Mexico, in collaboration with his brother Juan Jose Barragàn, is the first project of his career where the use of bold colour, which was to mark his particular interpretation of Mexican regionalism in his subsequent architectural production, was first expressed. The author of a book on Mexican architecture wrote: 'Of all the younger group, Barragàn has been most successful in his imaginative use of colour in modern architecture. His naturally sensitive aesthetic perceptions have never found satisfaction in restriction

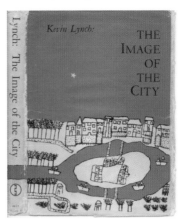

Fig.11
Cover of Kevin Lynch's *Image of the City*, Cambridge, MA, MIT Press, 1964.

47

25. Benjamin Spock, *Baby and Child Care* (New York: Dutton, 1997), 7th edition, first pub. 1946.
26. Steven W. Naifeh and Gregory White Smith, *Jackson Pollock: An American Saga*, New York, Harper Collins, 1991.
27. COBRA, no. 4, 1950. 28 Cobra 4, 1949. Quoted in W. Stockvis, *Cobra, Geschiedenis, voorspel en betekenis van een beweging in de kunst van na de tweede oorlog*, Amsterdam, De Bezige Bij, 1990. pp. 94-95.
29. Ibid..
30. Willem Sandberg, *Kunst en Kind*, Amsterdam, Stedelijk Museum, 1947
31. Lewis Mumford, *The American City*, Chicago, Oct., 1949. Quoted in *Goede Wonen*, Jan. 1950, p. 63.
32. Kevin Lynch, *The Image of the City* (Cambridge, MA.: The MIT Press, 1960).
33. Kevin Lynch (ed.) *Growing up in Cities, Studies of the Spatial Environment of Adolescence in Cracow, Melbourne, Mexico City, Salta, Toluca and Warszawa*, Cambridge, MA., MIT Press, 1977.

Fig.12
Le Corbusier,
rooftop playground
of the *Maison Unité
de Marseille*, 1946,
photo by USIS
Services Americains
d'information.

to the palette popularly associated with the International
Style. The most interesting things about the playground
are the triangular apertures which were common in
Mexican vernacular architecture, the colours ochre, red
and blue, the concrete umbrella pavilions with their
built in benches.'[34]

Regionalism was the characterizing feature of the
Hawaiian playgrounds of architect Harry Sims Brent in
Honolulu at around the same time. They were
implemented, like all his other works, in a style
appropriate to the island's tropical vegetation of palm,
pineapple and poinsettia trees and indigenous
architecture. Playground design also took another
regionalist twist with Dimitris Pikionis, the Greek
architect and landscape architect responsible for the
pathway to the Acropolis and the Philopappos Hill in
Athens between 1961 and 1964. He designed a
children's playground in a suburb of Athens called
Philothei. Here, by means of the construction of a
mythological, pre-Homeric past, he sought to enhance
a sense of place in children.[35]

Part of the empowerment of the child meant that some
of the greatest architects and artists channelled their
creativity to the design of playgrounds. Pierre Jeanneret
designed one for Chandigarh. And Le Corbusier
devoted almost one fifth of his plan for Chandigarh to a
recreational area. The so-called 'Valley of Leisure' there
is formed by a natural stream and links the lower parts
of the town to the upper ones. Footpaths alongside the
stream, which has been enlarged by a weir, lead to an
open-air theatre, cinema, rallying centres, platforms for
dancing, playgrounds, and other areas for leisure
activities.

The most striking playground of the period, however,
is the one Le Corbusier designed for the roof of the
Unité d'Habitation between 1946 and 1952. The open
roof terrace on the 17th floor of the Unité d'Habitation,
which contains 337 flats, was arranged as a children's
playground with a paddling pool, an outdoor stage, a
sports area, and a gymnasium. It also incorporates both
a kindergarten and a crèche. Through the functional
integration of the whole, a real community centre
emerged, which links not only the children of the Unité
but also the grown ups in sport, play and special
occasions. There was a windbreak on the eastern side,
a roof terrace with a stage wall, a flower bed, a
gymnasium, solaria, a children's playground, and a
wading pool (Fig.12).

Luis Barragàn, Isamu Noguchi designed a playground
in the 1930s.[36] In his autobiography, he notes that
throughout his career he had continually sought a way
'to bring sculpture into a more direct involvement with

the common experience of living'. His socializing impulse made him concerned with the fact that 'there must be a more direct way of contact than the rather remote one of art'. He was searching for 'a larger, more fundamentally sculptural purpose for sculpture, a more direct expression of man's relation to the earth and to his environment'. His first landscape project in 1933 took the form of a playground for children. On the opening page of his autobiography, he writes rather plaintively of his reaction as a child to a Japanese 'playground, or open space', which 'filled me with foreboding'. He saw the creation of space as 'an extension of sculpture'. Some of his early recollections bathe in retrospective melancholy, as he recalls his small-boy fears of a vacant landscape. 'It is possible that these impulses were already outlined in the *Sea Wave* I did as a child, or later conjured into the idea of a stage which would make its own music with the dance. *Play Mountain* and *The Monument to the Plough* were concepts out of which have flown so many of my hopeful proposals, such as the *Contoured Playground* and other playground and garden inventions.'

He wrote that he sought 'other means of communication – to find a way of sculpture that was humanly meaningful without being realistic, at once abstract and socially relevant'. *Play Mountain* was designed as a vast communal playground for a city block in Manhattan. It included a pool, a gymnasium, skating facilities, and a playground to be built in the shape of a gently sloping, tiered pyramid, housing a usable interior space. But it was turned down by NYC's Park Commissioner, Robert Moses, although it did lead to his 1940 project *Contoured Playground*.

In 1939, he was invited to Honolulu and the Park Commissioner, Lester McCoy, commissioned him to create playground equipment for Ala Moana Park, during the same period that Lewis Mumford was invited to develop a regional plan for that city.[37] For Noguchi, children's playgrounds came to symbolize a non-polemical means of projecting both his social and aesthetic interests without engaging in disturbing public controversy. 'For me, playgrounds are a way of creating the world.' And he described his *Play Mountain* as the prototype or 'kernel' for all his subsequent explorations 'relating sculpture to the earth'.

Of his initial interest in designing playgrounds and then

34. See I.E. Myers, *Mexico's Modern Architecture*, New York, Architecture Book Publ. Co., 1952, Esther Born, *Architecture in Mexico*, New York, Architectural Record, 1937, and Mark Trieb, 'El Pedregal', in F. Zanco (ed.), *Luis Barragan, the Quiet Revolution,* Milan, Skira, 2001, pp. 127-156.
35. Agni Pikioni, *Dimitris Pikionis*, vol 8: *The Children's Play Garden in Philothei, 1961-64,* Athens, Bastas-Plessas, 1994. 36 The following discussion is from Sam Hunter, *Isamu Noguchi*, London, Thames & Hudson, 1979, and from Isamu Noguchi, *Isamu Noguchi, A sculptor's World*, London, Thames and Hudson, 1967. See also Ana Maria Torres, *Isamu Noguchi, A Study of Space*, New York, Monacelli, 2000.
37. See Liane Lefaivre and Alex Tzonis, *Critical Regionalism*, Munich, Prestel, 2003. There we deal with Lewis Mumford's only real regional planning process, for Honolulu. He wrote about it in *Whither Honolulu?*

Fig.13
Isamu Noguchi and
Louis Kahn, *Bronze
Model (original in
plaster) of Fifth
Proposal*, November
1965.The fifth
design proposal for
the playground on
Riverside Drive,
produced at the end
of 1964,
encompassed a very
small area between
West 102nd and
West 103rd Streets.
Noguchi and Kahn
presented a
simplified version
that omitted
elements like the
central conical play
mountain
(by permission of the
Isamu Noguchi
Foundation and
Garden Museum).

more ambitious environments for adults, he wrote:
'Brancusi said that when an artist stopped being a child,
he would stop being an artist. Children, I think, view
the world differently from adults, their awareness of its
possibilities are more primary and attuned to their
capacities. When the adult would imagine like a child
he must project himself into seeing the world as a
totally new experience. I like to think of playgrounds as
a primer of shapes and functions; simple, mysterious,
and evocative: thus educational. The child's world
would be a beginning world, fresh and clear.'
When Honolulu Park Commissioner McCoy died,
Noguchi took the playground equipment designs to the
New York City Parks Department, where they were
rejected as potentially hazardous. With characteristic
ingenuity, he responded by designing an objectless
playground, eliminating sharp projections in favour of
curves and limiting the height of his forms to prevent
accidents. Nonetheless it was turned down and the city
was deprived of two great playgrounds: one for the
United Nations in 1952, and another that involved a
series of no less than five unexecuted designs for a
Riverside Drive park site. In Art News, Thomas B. Hess
deplored, in justifiable terms of outrage, the rejection of
Noguchi's imaginative U.N. design and Moses's
opposition: 'The playground, instead of telling the child
what to do (swing here, climb there), becomes a place
for endless exploration, of endless opportunity for
changing play. And it is a thing of beauty… in the
modern world.'[38]
The model was later exhibited in the children's
department of the MoMA as a protest. The Adele Levy
Memorial Playground for Riverside Drive was a
collaboration between Noguchi and Louis Kahn that
lasted 4 years, between 1958 and 1962. Kahn's interest
in playgrounds went back to 1943, when he had written
an article entitled 'Why City Planning is your
Responsibility' along with Oscar Stonorov. 'In most
urban areas, children play in the streets… There are too
many streets anyway. So why not make playgrounds out
of unnecessary streets?'[39] He and Noguchi submitted
five plans over a period of four years. The main
opposition came from the more affluent Riverside Drive
community, who feared an invasion of slum children
from nearby Broadway (Fig.13).
The project was rejected ultimately, but not before
Noguchi and Kahn had declared that 'we have
attempted to establish an area for familiar relaxation
and play rather than an area for any specific sport. We
have attempted to supply a landscape where children of
all ages, their parents and other older people can
mutually find enjoyment. The heart of the plan is a
nursery building placed as near to Riverside Drive as
possible which will supply the functions necessary to

lengthy sojourns in the park for little children. The
building is shaped like a cup, a sun trap for the winter
months, a fountain and water are for the summer. The
service and play rooms are built underneath the ramp
and under the open-air play and rest area so that the
roof has a double function. From this central point the
play area radiates with definite but not limiting forms
to invite play; first, integral with the nursery, is a play
mountain, like a mound of large triangular steps – for
climbing, for sitting – an artificial hill. Outside this
central core are giant slides built into the topography,
areas for home games, things to crawl in and out of.
There is also a large, oval sand and pebble area which
is criss-crossed by maze-like divisions: a theatre area
with a shell for music, puppets and theater.'[40]
Susan Solomon has written at length about another
episode in the history of post-war playgrounds: the
playground competition organized at the MoMA in
1954.[41] In that same year, Architectural Forum ran a
brief article on perhaps the most remarkable instance
of how all-pervasive the lure of playgrounds could be.
In 1950, a professional boxer by the name of Joe Brown
added the function of playground designer to his
already unusual mixture of associate professor of
boxing and sculpture at Princeton University. Students
of architecture had been asked to design a playground
and he was asked to judge it. He criticized their work
as unrelated to human needs, unimaginative and overly
imitative of the Scandinavia school of 'play sculpture'.
When the graduate students asked Professor Brown for
his credentials in this field, he replied 'I was a boy
once'. Then he designed his own playgrounds and
4 years later, in 1954, he delivered a paper in St Louis
to a meeting of the National Recreation Association and
exhibited models which would help 'to prepare children
for the struggles of maturity'. Perhaps because he was
a boxer, he included an element of danger in the
playgrounds. They did indeed incorporate an element
of unpredictability. He called his apparatus a play
'community' because 'any child who uses it is forced
by circumstance to recognize the vitality of his
surroundings. Through experience he is taught to
respect the complexity of every situation even though
his personal aims might be simple. This respect will be
neither unreasonable fear nor a thoughtless sense of
security – just an acceptance of the fact that personal
designs and social designs are interdependent. The

38. *Art News*, April 1952, quoted in Ibid.
39. Louis Kahn and Oskar Stonorov, 'Why Urban Planning is your Responsibility',
Revere's Part in Better Living, 17, 1943, pp. 6-7. 40 Isamu Noguchi, *Isamu Noguchi;
A Sculptor's World*, London, Thames & Hudson, 1967.
40. Isamu Noguchi, *Isamu Noguchi;A sculptor's World*, London, Thames & Hudson,
1967.
41. Susan Solomon, *American Playgrounds, Revitalizing Community Space*,
University Press of New England, Lebanon, 2005. The MoMA competition was co-
sponsored by Frank Caplan, the founder of a playground furniture company, Creative
Playthings.

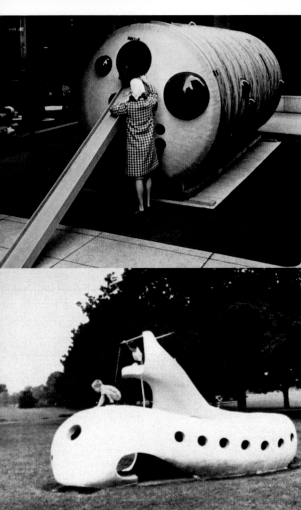

factor of unpredictability – the creative factor – places upon the child the responsibility – at this time in life, the fun – of choosing, of emerging, of choosing again, of emerging again, ad infinitum.' He even waxed quasi-poetic: 'Practice in the art of living, the rare art of accepting each accomplishment as a signpost in a wonderful journey that never ends; a journey made on one vehicle – a mind and body, one and inseparable.'[42] (Figs.14-16)

After the Rise:
Jane Jacobs and Playground Dystopia

For a while, during the 1940s and 50s, it looked like there was no end in sight for the optimism and feel-good factor that surrounded playground design. But if playgrounds had managed to inspire such optimism in such prominent figures as Lewis Mumford, the Goodman brothers, Le Corbusier, Noguchi and Kahn at the time, 1964 can be seen as marking the end of the enthusiasm. This is when Jane Jacobs published her famous *The Death and Life of Great American Cities*. This book contained a chapter 'The Uses of Sidewalks: Assimilating Children' and it was one long tirade against playgrounds. 'Among the superstitions of planning and housing is a fantasy about the transformation of children,' she wrote. 'It goes like this: a population of children is condemned to play on city streets. These pale and rickety children, in their sinister moral environment, are telling each other canards about sex, sniggering evilly, and learning new forms of corruption as efficiently as if they were in reform school. This situation is called "moral and physical toll taken of our youth by the streets," sometimes it is called simply "the gutter".'

'If only these deprived children can be gotten off the streets into parks and playgrounds with equipment on which to exercise, space in which to run, grass to lift their souls! Clean and happy places, filled with the laughter of children responding to a wholesome environment. So much for the fantasy,' she continued. She reported that 'street gangs do their street fighting predominantly in parks and playgrounds. When the New York Times in September 1959 summed up the worst adolescent gang outbreaks of the past decade in the city, each and every one was designated as having occurred in a park.' Her main criticism was that play had been divorced from streets. She reports that her son told her 'I was scared they would catch me when I had to pass the playground. If they caught me there I'd be sunk.'

The disaster of playgrounds was grave, involving violent crime. 'A few days after the murder of two sixteen-year-old boys in a playground on the midtown

Fig.14
Jerry Lieberman, *Plastic Playthings of the Pepsi-Cola Indoor Playground*, New York City, USA, undated, photo by Thecla, New York.

Fig.15
Joseph Brown, *Play sculptures with Climbing Nets*, Princeton University, Princeton, USA, unattributed photo.

West Side of Manhattan, I paid a morbid visit to the area,' she wrote. 'The nearby streets were evidently back to normal. Hundreds of children, directly under the eyes of innumerable adults using the sidewalks themselves and looking from windows, were engaged in a vast variety of sidewalk games and whooping pursuits. The sidewalks were dirty, they were too narrow, but there was no scene of arson, mayhem, or of flourishing of dangerous weapons. In the playground where the night-time murder had occurred, things were back to normal too. Three small boys were setting fire under a wooden bench. Another was having his head beaten against the concrete. The custodian was absorbed in solemnly and slowly hauling down the American flag.'

She includes garden city planners in her critique, quoting a 1928 Regional Plan Association of New York report. 'Careful checking within a radius of 1/4 miles of playgrounds under a wide range of conditions in many cities shows that only about 1/7 of the child population from 5 to 15 years of age may be found on these grounds. …The lure of the street is a strong competitor …It must be a well-administered playground to compete successfully with the city streets, teeming with life and adventure. This ability to make playground activity so compellingly attractive as to draw the children from the streets to hold their interest from day to day is a rare faculty in play leadership, combining personality and technical skill of a high order.'

Better to play in the streets than in a playground is the conclusion she drew. 'On my way home, as I passed the relatively genteel playground near where I live, I noted that its only inhabitants in the late afternoon, with the mothers and the custodian gone, were two small boys threatening to bash a little girl with their skates, and an alcoholic who had roused themselves to shake his head and mumble they shouldn't do that. Farther down the street on a block with many Puerto Rican immigrants, was another scene of contrast. Twenty-eight children of all ages were playing on the sidewalk without mayhem, arson, or any event more serious than a squabble over a bag of candy. Arriving home I noticed that at the end of our block, in front of the tenement, the tailor's, our house, the laundry, the pizza place and the fruit man's, twelve children were playing on the sidewalk in sight of fourteen adults.'[43]

Jane Jacobs was only stating what had become obvious by the early 1960s. The fact was that Lewis Mumford, Noguchi, and Kahn had been naïve. The optimistic playground visions of the post-war period were indeed built largely on 'fantasy', as she put it. The hard reality

a new dimension in playground planning!

Creative Playthings, Inc., pioneers in the development of play materials for early childhood education, now offers a *complete playground planning, design and building service* through its newly-formed Play Sculpture Division.

On its staff are leading designers, sculptors, engineers, educators and landscape architects, including such well-known names as Isamu Noguchi, E. Moller-Nielsen (Sweden), Robert Winston, A. Vitali (Switzerland), etc.

The Play Sculpture Division is currently co-sponsoring—together with the *Museum of Modern Art and Parents' Magazine*—a nationwide Play Sculpture Competition.

Play Sculpture Division maintains a permanent display and resource center at 5 University Place, New York. You are cordially invited also to visit our exhibit at the forthcoming National Recreation Congress in Philadelphia.

We invite your inspection and inquiry.

Full descriptive literature will be sent you on request.

PLAY SCULPTURES DIVISION

CREATIVE PLAYTHINGS, INC., 5 UNIVERSITY PLACE
NEW YORK 3, N. Y. • ORegon 4-7858

September 1953   When writing to our advertisers please mention Recreation.   201

Fig.16
Advertisement, Sept. 1953, by Creative Playthings announcing its nationwide play sculpture competition, co-sponsored by the MoMA.

53

42. "Playground sculpture – for the fun of it," *Architectural Forum*, November 1954, p. 157.
43. Jane Jacobs, *The Death and Life of Great American Cities*, New York, Vintage, 1961, pp. 79-82.

Fig.17
Cornelis van
Eesteren, Plan for
the Expansion of
Amsterdam (1932),
Amsterdam Planning
Department, directed
by Van Eesteren.
Northern elevation
of the city viewed
from the south-east
in aerial perspective
(by permission of the
NAi).

54

of street violence and crime put an end to them before they even got off the drawing board and into real urban environments. Noguchi's playgrounds are a case in point. For all their good intentions and universally recognized merits as sculpture, they found no support, either in the municipal administration or among the public.

Social Concerns:
Urban Villages, Streets, and Polycentric Nets

At the beginning of this text, I mentioned that there is almost no one today in the field of architecture or urbanism who is actively involved in creating community, in bringing people together, in the quality of public space. This was not true in the period following World War II up to the early 1970s. Jane Jacobs was among the most outspoken members of a new, post-World War II group of urban theoreticians and writers who were critical of the authoritarian, regimenting approaches to urbanism, in particular the technocratic, big-government policies that had fuelled CIAM's visions. Her generation, taking its cue from the pioneering Chicago School of Urban Sociology, particularly Louis Wirth, who, in his *Urbanism as a Way of Life*, analysed the city in terms of its impact on people, pointed to the alienation and anomie of urban life.[44]

Jane Jacobs's generation was more attached to the 'dirty real' aspects of urban life than the Utopian, visionary ones. As a result, their approach was bottom-up rather than top-down. They were fired by issues of populist architecture and urbanism as a means, not of replacing, but of tempering the technocratic and bureaucratic government policies with new ones, involving democratic techniques based on participation, consensus, inclusion and equitability, as a means of coping in a responsible way with the new, complex social realities of post-1945 world.[45]

The post-war period came to be characterized, not only in Amsterdam but in Europe generally, by a new kind of urban design. It was bent on finding an alternative to the regimenting approach, oblivious to the small, ordinary realities of everyday life. It was characterized by disenchantment with ambitious, large-scale systems and, instead, by a concern for ways of enhancing community. This was the beginning of what Alex Tzonis has elsewhere referred to as the 'humanist rebellion'.[46]

Indeed, before WWII, there was only one kind of modern urban planning that was acceptable to the avant-garde architectural profession: one that imposed its regimenting, normative framework on the city in a top-down manner. Four of the major figures of the time, all members of the then most professionally powerful group of architects and town planners, CIAM (Congrès Internationaux d'Architecture Moderne), used different wojrds to describe this type of planning. Victor Bourgeois referred to it as 'rationelle Behauungs-weisen',[47] Le Corbusier as 'La Cité Radieuse',[48] Ludwig Hilberseimer as 'Grosstadt Architektur',[49] and Cornelis van Eesteren as the 'Functionele Stad'.[50] No other image encapsulates better idea of the strategy shared by CIAM than the famous photograph of Le Corbusier's hand gesturing towards a model of his Cité Radieuse, in an imperious, impersonal, detached way.

The most radical change that affected the thinking about cities in the aftermath of the Second World War consisted of inverting this top-down CIAM approach to urbanism and adopting an approach that was bottom-up. Two images sum up the revolution in the urban-design profession's approach to the city. One is Van Eesteren's Extension Plan of Amsterdam of 1934, with its sweeping standardization and regimenting blocks. The other is the post-war map with the insertion of some post-war playgrounds into the fabric of the Jordaan neighbourhood of Amsterdam.[51] (Figs.17-20) Even more intimately related to the world of city planning and architecture was the work of urban geographer Pierre Henri Chombart de Lauwe's *Paris et l'agglomération parisienne*.[52] This was first sociological study of post-war peripheral Paris. Like Lefebvre, Chombart discovered a new way of looking at the built environment, discovering new objects that had been ignored by urban planners in France. More specifically, he redefined the boundaries and the parcels of a city as these were understood by the various inhabitants beyond the technical categories applied up to that time. Perhaps in the way they combine top-down with bottom-up, the Amsterdam playgrounds come closest to Norbert Wiener's cybernetic theory of self-regulating organisms, constantly adjusting themselves in response to new inputs. They 'learn from' their evolving contexts through, as we shall see, a highly active, democratic, participatory feedback process that is characteristic of the city of Amsterdam.[53] The first to look at this bottom-up thinking after WWII had been Henri Lefebvre. His *Critique de la vie*

44. Louis Firth, *Urbanism as a Way of Life*, American Journal of Sociology, vol. 44, no. 1 (July 1938), pp. 1-24.
45. These issues are dealt with in Alexander Tzonis and Liane Lefaivre 'In the Name of the People: The Populist Movement in Architecture', *Forum* (Dutch) 1976 (Special Issue).
46. Liane Lefaivre and Alex Tzonis, *Aldo van Eyck, Humanist Rebel; In-Betweening in a Postwar World*, Rotterdam, 010, 1999 47 Report by CIAM, Stuttgart 1931;
48. Le Corbusier, *Oeuvre Complete*
49. Ludwig Hilberseimer, *Grosstadt Architecture*, Stuttgart, 1927.
50. See Vincent van Rossem, p 153.
51. See Lefaivre and Tzonis, *Aldo van Eyck, Humanist Rebel*, Rotterdam, 010, 1999.
52. Pierre Henri Chombart de Lauwe, *Paris et l'agglomeration parisienne* (Paris, PUF, 1952).
53. Norbert Wiener *Cybernetics of Control and Communication in the Animal and Machine*, 1948

Figs.18-20 Maps indicating location of interstitial play-grounds for the centre of Amster-dam, early 1950s (with kind permission of the Municipal Archives, Amsterdam).

quotidienne (1947) argued that the ordinary, forgotten, everyday areas of normal rather than affluent shoppers on the periphery of the elite, metropolitan city were privileged places of poetic experience and social life. Lefebvre's book outlined the theory of 'everydayness', 'le quotidien', built around the potentials of the humble and repetitive aspects of life, as opposed to those related either to the world of production or consumption. Here, he asserted the 'right' to the city as a place of pleasure and enjoyment, independent of the imperatives of the economy. More precisely, he saw the city as the locus of 'festival'. His purpose was 'to oppose everyday life and re-organize it until it is as good as new, its spurious rationality and authority unmasked and the antithesis between the quotidian and the Festival exposed'.[54] A good city, like a good civilization, was one that integrated play into its human and social fabric. The kind of urban environment Lefebvre was talking about was not the traditional heart of the city, the 'high' sections of the city boulevards, downtown, public squares. It was the popular neighborhoods, blue collar, what Aragon had called 'les paysans de Paris',[55] the *banlieux* photographed by Robert Doisneau.

Besides Lefebvre, the existentialist writings of Jean-Paul Sartre, perhaps the most popular philosopher internationally at that moment and certainly the one with the biggest influence, also played a role in grounding a new bottom-up approach.[56] In his own way, he rebelled like Lefebvre against the idea of grandiose, top-down, authoritarian systems. To Sartre, they suffered from 'the illusion of immanence', the attachment to some grand all-embracing, abstract metaphysical system. Accordingly, he challenged his contemporaries, particularly the younger post-war generation, to become 'engaged in the world', and in its unique 'situations'.[57] This was also very much the attitude that prevailed among the discontent, upstart anti-heroes of the generalized post-war rebellion against the traditional, conformist, 'big bluff' cultural values, manifested in England by John Osborne's proto-counter-cultural 'angry young man', in France by Albert Camus's *L'Homme révolté*, and in the USA by Nicholas Ray's *Rebel Without a Cause*.[58]

In the same vein as Lefebvre and Sartre, Jane Jacobs and her generation chose as their target top-down, authoritarian public space, that is, the kind of city centre embraced by CIAM and, before it, the City Beautiful movement. Jacobs called such designs nothing but an 'orgiastic assemblage of rich buildings' made up of 'one grandiose monument after another'. She accused them of not being a 'public success'. Their failure lay in the fact that, although 'people tended to be proud of them', 'they still didn't use them'.[59] In other words, they did not enhance the sense of community that was the essence of urban life. They did nothing to allay the growing feeling that social life in cities was that of a 'lonely crowd'.

David Riesman was the person who coined this term. The main concern of his book, *The Lonely Crowd* (1950), the biggest-selling sociological study in history, was that traditional forms of community have been replaced by the 'lonely crowd' made up of 'other directed' types – personalities necessary for the smooth running of big anonymous corporations and organiza-tions, persons who were at home anywhere and nowhere, superficially affable and conformist, but deeply anxious and isolated.[60]

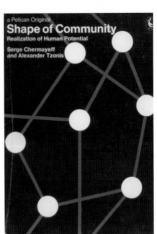

Fig.21
Cover of Serge Chermayeff and Alexander Tzonis, *Shape of Community*, 1972.

Indeed, community became the main concern of this generation of writers and the search to enhance community became the task of everyone interested in the subject of architecture and the city. Community became the lifelong aim of Aldo van Eyck's projects under the concept of what he famously called the 'Realm of the In-between'.[61] As far back as the early 1950s, Peter and Alison Smithson were perhaps influenced by the photographs of London's working class by Nigel Henderson about the time they were working on their Robin Hood Lane housing project.[62] Jane Jacobs, for her part, defended the importance of maintaining traditional, everyday, small-scale, interstitial urban spaces – basically the street – as a means of maintaining community. She is still remembered most today for her successful campaign as one of the community leaders of Lower Manhattan against the planned demolition in the mid 1960s. Community became a catchword of some of the most popular, best-selling books on the city: Paul and Percival Goodman's *Communitas*,[63] Serge Chermayeff and Christopher Alexander's *Community and Privacy*, Serge Chermayeff and Alexander Tzonis's *Shape of Community*, for example.[64] (Fig.21) The sociologist Herbert Gans produced two key works in this respect. *The Levittowners* painted a positive picture of life of community in the new suburbs, upsetting commonplace

57

54. Henri Lefebvre, *Everyday Life in the Modern World* (New York: Harper, 1971) pp. 205-206.
55. Louis Aragon, *Le Paysan de Paris*, 1926
56. See Lefaivre and Tzonis *Aldo van Eyck, Humanist Rebel*, Rotterdam, 010, 1999.
57. Jean-Paul Sartre, *L'Etre et le néant*, Paris, Gallimard, 1943.
58. John Osborne, *Look back in Anger*; Albert Camus, *L'homme révolté*; and Nicolas Rays *Rebel without a Cause*. 59 Jane Jacobs, *The Rise and Fall of Great American Cities*, New York, Vintage, 1961.
60. David Riesman and Nathan Glazer, *The Lonely Crowd*, New York, 1950. Although Glazer is listed as the co-author he has often stated that the real author is Riesman.
61. See Liane Lefaivre and Alexander Tzonis, *Aldo van Eyck, Humanist Rebel, In-Betweening in a Postwar World*, Rotterdam, 010, 1999.
62. Victoria Walsh, *Nigel Henderson, Parallel of Art and Life*, introduced by Peter Smithson. London, Thames and Hudson, 2001.
63. Paul and Percival Goodman, *Communitas*, Chicago, Univ. of Chicago Press, 1947
64. Paul and Percival Goodman, *Communitas* Chicago, Univ. of Chicago Press, 1947. This discussion is taken from Liane Lefaivre, Alexander Tzonis and Richard Diamond, *Architecture in North America since 1960*, London, Thames & Hudson, 1996..

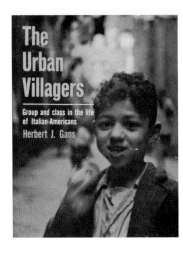

Fig.22
Herbert J. Gans,
The Urban Villagers;
group and class in
the life of Italian-
Americans. Free
Press of Glencoe,
New York 1962.

notions about suburbia fostering anomie and loneliness. Gans's *The Urban Villagers*, a sociological study of the working-class, Italian neighbourhood of Boston's West End, caused a sensation by arguing that the poor, working-class neighbourhood was superior to a new project of urban renewal plan because it was based on strong community ties.[65] (Fig.22)

Practitioners took these ideas and put them into operation with participatory design processes in real neighbourhoods in the 1960s. Paul Davidoff, Robert Goodman, Chester Hartman, Phyllis Lambert, who were part of a group of participation and advocacy planners, went even further, arguing for the importance of people power and of architects taking to the streets and working with real-life communities in the design of their architectural and urban environments.[66] (Fig.23) Others devised other design tools to implement the idea of community. The most ingenious, in my view, was what Kevin Lynch would call the 'polycentered net'.[67] The earliest exponent is Louis Kahn's *Philadelphia Plan*. The net is evident in many of Team Ten's projects, as in the Smithson's plan for Cambridge, for example, and in Giancarlo de Carlo's plan for Urbino. The most systematic and fruitful application of this was in the projects actually implemented by Shadrach Woods, based on his version of the net, which he called the 'web'. His plan for the Free University of Berlin is, arguably, the most sophisticated application of the idea.[68] Still others proposed a piecemeal, incremental, interstitial approach to urban renovation as an alternative to large-scale urban renovation schemes. This approach is most often associated with the work of Aldo van Eyck, particularly his *Home for Unwed Parents* in Amsterdam (1972) – which is not surprising in view of his part in the interstitially located Amsterdam playground.

The Amsterdam Playgrounds:
Bringing a City Together after a War

It was 1945. The war had just ended. People celebrated, as did children. In the war-torn city there were few places to play (Figs.24, 25)

The Amsterdam playgrounds have a lot in common with the projects we have looked at – involving play and community. What made them unique, however, and what explains their unique success was that they were not conceived as isolated, one-off, individual playgrounds. On the contrary, the Amsterdam playgrounds were part of a bottom-up, integrated urban planning process. They formed a polycentric net of public spaces around which community formed, creating micro-urban villages. These did not disrupt the

Fig.23
Cover of Paul
Goodman, *After the
Planners*, 1971.

urban tissue around them. On the contrary, they were inserted into the left-over spaces, the empty interstices. Moreover, they used techniques of democratic participation. The archives of the city of Amsterdam contain over 190 letters from the citizens of Amsterdam requesting a playground. The countless memos, passed from hand to hand in the city administration, covered with the signatures of one civil employee after another, from department to department, reveal the enormous and meticulous work performed by civil servants for the city. These, and the letters, testify to a kind of support that was nothing short of phenomenal, both on behalf of the municipal government and on behalf of the people of Amsterdam.[69] (Figs. 26)

These post-war playgrounds, built in a period of just over 20 years, revolutionized the design of playgrounds. The claim here is that what makes them unique – even today – are three characteristics: they were not imposed from above by a city administration but part of a 'people power' participatory process involving the citizens and the Urban Development department of Amsterdam; they were not placed on a piece of land cleared for that purpose but inserted in interstices within the living urban fabric; they were designed not as individual units, but as part of an extended polycentered network of playgrounds.

This new approach to playgrounds – participatory, interstitial and polycentric – is not just revolutionary in the design of playgrounds but in the design of public space in general. This approach is based on what we choose to call the 'PIP principle' (Polycentric, Interstitial, Participatory Public Space). It can be said that Amsterdam playgrounds were the first example, not only of a new type of playground design, but also, in general, of a new approach to public space and a new urban design that emerged in the post-war period, where public space was conceived of as a distributed network, a polycentric net.

The creation of this new type of public space owed its emergence to the designer of the individual playgrounds, Aldo van Eyck. He is the most well known, of course, but the credit must be assigned equally – if not more – to Cornelis van Eesteren, Jacoba Mulder and the Public Works Department and the people of

Fig.24
End of the war, children celebrating on the Oudezijds Achterburgwal, 1945. Photo by Emmy Andriesse (by permission of Leiden University Library).

Fig.25
Children playing on the Rapenburgerstraat in Amsterdam, 1950s. Photo by Rolf Kruger (by permission of Leiden University Library).

59

Fig.26
Letter from a citizen of Amsterdam to Cornelis van Eesteren, requesting a playground, 1947.

65. Herbert Gans, *The Urban Villagers, Group and Class in the Life of Italian Americans*, New York, Free Press, 1962 and *The Levittowners, Life and Politics in the New Suburban Community*, New York, Free Press, 1967.
66. 1967. For a history of the rise of what we have called the populist movement in architecture, to which all these authors belong, see Alexander Tzonis and Liane Lefaivre, 'In the Name of the People. The Populist Movement in Architecture', in Michael Shamiyeh, *What the People Want*, Basel, Birkhauser, 2005, pp. 270-305. See also the interview of Phyllis Lambert by Liane Lefaivre in the *Harvard Design Review* entitled 'Phyllis Lambert, Advocacy Planner of the late 1960s', pp. 83-86.
67. Kevin Lynch, quoted in Liane Lefaivre, 'Space, Place and Play', *Aldo van Eyck, The Playgrounds and the City*, Amsterdam, Stedelijk Museum, 2002.
68. See Alexander Tzonis and Liane Lefaivre, 'After the Monuments; Shadrach Woods' Free University', *Free University Berlin*, London, A.A., 1999, pp. 118-140. 69 Municipal Archives.

Fig.27a-d
Aldo van Eyck,
before and after
shots of his play-
grounds in the
historic inner city
of Amsterdam:
Conraedstraat
(above), then
Dijkstraat (right)
(by permission of the
Municipal Archives,
Amsterdam).

Amsterdam. The way they converged is essential to the way the playgrounds fell into place. If one of these actors had been missing, it is doubtful that the playgrounds and shape of the particular public realm they created would have materialized.

Aldo van Eyck

The fact that Aldo van Eyck was interested in designing for children hardly bears repeating, particularly as he wrote about it so much himself. His only book (although never published) was *The Child, the City and the Poet*.[70] As a close collaborator of COBRA – he was commissioned to install their above-mentioned 1949 exhibition at the Stedelijk – Van Eyck's attachment to childhood is not surprising. His architectural renderings in children's crayons of some of the playgrounds share something else with COBRA art. Like these artists, who were trying to imitate children in their drawing style, as Corneille's *Promenade au Pays des Pommes* reveals, Aldo van Eyck also used children's coloured pencils in his renderings of the playgrounds. An indication of just how much Aldo van Eyck identified with the Expressionist paintings of the COBRA group is the highly publicized scandal he provoked by his outrage in defence of a painting called 'The Questioning Children' (1949), which was in danger of being painted over after Appel had painted it in the Amsterdam Town Hall.[71] Aldo van Eyck was almost fired by his superiors over the scandal.

That Van Eyck's interest in childhood influenced one of the main figures of the group, Constant, is clear.[72] Indeed, the artist claims that he told Aldo van Eyck that he wanted to become an architect, to which Aldo responded by lending him all his class notebooks from his time at the ETH in Zurich, assuring him that this was sufficient.[73] He indirectly gave Constant jobs by introducing him to his superior at the Public Works Department, Jacoba Mulder, who, in turn, bought sculptures from Constant and commissioned him to design some play structures for some playgrounds, particularly Sarphati Park.[74] Constant and Van Eyck went on to do a joint exhibition on spatial colourism at the Stedelijk in 1952, and Constant's counter-Utopian *Babylon* project owes a great debt to Van Eyck's playgrounds, not to mention his own sculpture entitled *Ambiance de jeu* (1956).[75] In at least one case, the Dijkstraat playground of 1954, Aldo van Eyck created a work of art and a playground simultaneously. It was conceived within the context of the site, and gives a frame to urban life. As opposed to the more traditional post-war public sculptures in Rotterdam – by Picasso, Gabo, Moore or Zadkine – which were conceived as monuments to be looked at in isolation from their surroundings, the playgrounds 'learn' from their context. It is one of the first site-specific sculptures in the post-war period. In its density of meaning and impact on the urban setting, it recalls the type of urban sculpture that Richard Serra, James Turrel, and Christo would build – but almost twenty years later. From this point of view, it is like Kurt Schwitters's *Merzbarn* (1947), a sculpture carved into an existing dilapidated building in Newcastle-upon-Tyne.[76] In addition, it is one of the unique cases where the same work is good at being two things – urbanism and sculpture – simultaneously. They are readable in both registers. They overlap completely. In addition, they are masterpieces in both cases.

Almost everything Van Eyck built involved designing for children. Among the first projects he designed were the Amsterdam playgrounds, the school in Nagele, and the Amsterdam Orphanage – all for children. He chose to have his projects photographed with children in them, like the Amsterdam Orphanage with the famous photographs by Violette Cornelius. Even Sonsbeek, an open-air art gallery destined for adult visitors, was photographed with children visiting it. Every one of his articles mentions children. Ultimately there is no better proof of his devotion to children than the fact that he personally and painstakingly designed 770 playgrounds along with the play furniture they contain. (Figs.28a-f) Yet, nowhere in the writings of Aldo van Eyck is there a sign that he ever thought of any of his playgrounds as anything but individual pieces. From this point of view, his playgrounds are not fundamentally different in their approach than those of other architects we have reviewed. Two people are responsible for the new, urban approach embodied ion the Amsterdam playgrounds: Cornelis van Eesteren and Jacoba Mulder.

Cornelis van Eesteren

Cornelis van Eesteren is less often associated with the Amsterdam playgrounds than Aldo van Eyck. In fact, he is generally looked upon as one of the staunchest defenders of the regimenting, authoritarian, top-down approach to the city as propounded by the pre-war CIAM. However, after the war he changed his views dramatically.[77] He underwent what might be termed a 'humanist rebel transformation'. This former top-down, arch-functionalist became a devoted supporter of the bottom-up, participatory approach to urban planning.

70. Aldo van Eyck, *The Child, the City and the Poet,* unpublished manuscript.
71. See W.J.H.B. Sandberg, A.D. Petersen, Pieter Brattinga (eds.) *Sandberg, een documentaire,* Amsterdam, Kosmos, 1975, pp. 60-61.
72. Letter from Walraven, dated 1949.
73. Telephone conversation with the author, 11 March 2002.
74. Ibid.75 Lefaivre and Tzonis, op. cit.59-61.
76. Lefaivre and Tzonis, p. 52-54.
77. Vincent van Rossum presents him this way in *Van Eesteren, Het algemeen Uitbredingsplan van Amsterdam,* Amsterdam, 1991. See also Julian Galindo Gonzalez, *Cornelis van Eesteren, La Experiencia de Amsterdam 1929-1958,* Barcelona, Arquitesis, 2003.

As City Development Director for the Public Works Department of the City of Amsterdam, he changed in his approach radically and, as recent research into the Municipal Archives has shown, this was directly due to the Amsterdam playgrounds.[78] Without abandoning the idea of top-down planning, he began to 'learn' from the particularities and irregularities of residual, interstitial places in the existing fabric of the city to and work with them rather than ignore them. His about-face is remarkable. It is he who came up with the polycentric, interstitial, participatory concept of the Amsterdam playgrounds.

Even before the end of the war, he mentions playgrounds in one of his memos dated 25 September 1944.[79] This is the beginning of an interest that will remain with him for the rest of his professional life as head of Urban Development. This planner who, before the war, had represented his plans for the extension of Amsterdam with top-down, bird's-eye views of the city, became actively concerned about the smallest details of playgrounds, notably the shape of particular sand-boxes, the location of a particular playgrounds, and the reactions of citizens to them.[80]

It is hard to believe that a planner who, before the war had been thinking of the city exclusively in terms of distant, massive, featureless expanses of blank blocks, would send a memo marked 'urgent' concerning the lowly profile of concrete a sand pit on the Manenburgstraat. Yet this is what happened on 16 September 1948.[81] Van Eesteren himself sent a note about the future of the playground on the Goudriaanstraat on 26 February 1951, indicating that he played an active role in its design.[82] In another memo dated 25 January 1952, to the head engineer, once again about the profile of a sandpit, he expresses a liking for the Bertelmanplein model.[83] He personally orders the playground on the Gordijnensteeg,[84] and later the playground in the Haarlemmermeerkwartier, on the Legmeerplein, and the Jacob Marisplein.[85] On 17 February 1954, he writes a long letter about the playgrounds being considered for the Korte Leidsedwarsstraat, Lange Leidsedwarsstraat, Leidse Kruisstraat, Lange Leidsedwarsstraat, and Noorderstraat.[86] On 2 February 1954 he leaves his signature on Van Eyck's letter about the playground on Hogendorpstraat. An indication of how closely he was involved with Van Eyck and the playgrounds is that he writes on 20 March 1954 that he agrees with the changes of the play furniture. 'There must be a clear contrast between space and the area to be used for play. I request you to discuss it with architect Van Eijck in these terms.'[87]

The countless memos, all signed and countersigned by often seven or eight civil servants of the Public Works Department, now in the playground archive of the Amsterdam Municipal Archives, are proof of Van Eesteren's unflagging concern. He was in many ways, in fact, party to the smallest details of the playgrounds. On 7 June 1954, Van Eesteren personally answers a letter of a citizen of Amsterdam, a certain Mrs. Padt-Luckens, who wants a playground in her neighbour-hood.[88] Amazingly, we find him, the head of urban planning of an entire city, bothering about the size and shape of a sand pit! In a letter dated 7 April 1954, he complains that the playground for the Iepenplein is too small.[89] On 3 May 1954, he sends a personal memo ordering playgrounds in de Jordaan as part of a restructuring plan.[90] He also specifies how important the playgrounds on the Leliedwarsstraat, Rozenstraat, Lijnbaansgracht, Laurierstraat, and Egelantierstraat are to his urban plan. 'In connection with this, any playgrounds to be established could only be regarded as being temporary,' he writes.[91] On 15 May 1954,[92] he sends an astonishingly detailed note regarding the different aspects of the Smaragdstraat playground. 'The central strip of the Smaragdstraat does not seem to me to be suitable for creating a playground. The park on the Granaatstraat must be maintained due to its very typical character. [...] It would not appear opportune to reduce road area, but perhaps some playing equipment could be placed on the central island, which will also stop cars being parked there. In view of the fact that it (the grounds, ed.) are rather large, it seems to me to be appropriate to establish a playground here. [...] The area on the Hemonystraat [...] is situated on busy traffic roads. I believe it would be dangerous to lay out this area for small children.'

But these playgrounds were not only remarkable for the minute attention with which Van Eesteren and Van Eyck dealt with the smallest details of the playgrounds. More importantly, they were highly innovative from the point of view of urban planning and design. They were innovative in four senses:
First, Van Eesteren allowed for the playgrounds to be interstitially implanted in the in-between spaces left

78. See the uninventorized archives entitled *Speelplaatsen* and *Zandspeelplatseen*.
79. No 519 dd
80. See archive
81. 20b
82. 136
83. 141 a
84. 319 a
85. 398 a
86. 406a
87. 399a
88. 471a
89. 430a
90. 443
91. 447
92. 451

over in the traditional urban fabric of the city of Amsterdam. Nothing had to be knocked down to make way for them. Bertelmanplein, for example, was simply inserted into an existing leafy, picturesque nineteenth-century square. The Hasebroekstraat playground (1954/55) was built on the site of a urinal at an intersection of two streets on the edge of a canal. The Van Hogendorpplein playground was located on a traffic roundabout. The Boetzelaerstraat playground arose in the middle of a traffic junction, and the Rapen-burgh and Laurier playgrounds on dump sites. The fact that they were interstitial also meant they were by definition expendable and that the parcels could be re-used if the playgrounds outlived their purpose. Today, only the playgrounds that still have a group of children still using them exist. Others have been integrated into the larger urban fabric. Out of forty playgrounds that I observed in 2003, only about half were still play-grounds. Others had been turned into a supermarket, one into a Chinese Temple, one into a house, one into a traffic intersection, one into a whorehouse.[93]

Second, the fact that they were interstitial meant the playgrounds were much smaller than the standard ones, but also that there were many more of them, and they made up a far more tightly-knit polycentered network than is usually the case. In a period of about twenty years, from the time of the first playground in 1947 to 1968, in fact, Van Eesteren gave the permission for no fewer than a thousand playgrounds to be built in Amsterdam, thus creating another city

Third, they were participatory. Each one was the result of a personal written request on the part of a citizen which was inspected and evaluated by Van Eesteren's department in the Publics Works Department, often by Van Eesteren himself – at least in the beginning. We know this from the internal memos that have been kept in the Municipal Archive of the City of Amsterdam. For example, the memo of 10 November 1949 covers the first 12 playgrounds that had been implanted in the city.[94]

Fourth, Van Eesteren took the first, second and third features of the playgrounds that had emerged ad-hoc in the traditional fabric of Amsterdam – interstitiality, polycentricity and participation – and made them into a design tool that he then applied in his designs for the new post-war neighbourhoods of West Amsterdam, Sloterdijk, Slotermeer, and Geuzeveld. The fact that the playgrounds became an integral part of his planning of the new towns of West Amsterdam probably goes a long way in explaining the quality of life in these neighbourhoods.[95]

But what actually made Van Eesteren change his mind so radically? What turned him from a staunch CIAM defender of the 'functionele stad' to such an apparently soft-hearted, sentimental obsessed with the tiny details of everyday life?

A meeting at the RIBA in 1946; CIAM dismissed

One event offers an insight into the transition between the pre-war CIAM and the post-war rebel humanist phase of Van Eesteren's career. There is an article in his archive, dated February 1946.[96] It contains the minutes of a meeting in London in which English architects convened at the RIBA to attend his presentation of his new expansion plan for the West of Amsterdam. As is clear from their remarks, the English architects belong to the tradition of Ebenezer Howard and Raymond Unwin's Garden City movement, and are sympathetic to Regional Planning ideas. With regard to Van Eesteren's plan, designed according to the CIAM principles of strip housing, there is one prolonged attack by W.G. Holford which is negative in the extreme. 'It must be very difficult,' the speaker states, 'to conjure up the fantastic and to get variety in those conditions (density), especially if you are a man with a scientific philosophic attitude as Mr Van Eesteren is. Personally I do not like over-rigidity.' The English architect in question goes on to point out to Van Eesteren in the most pointed manner possible that there is a 'need to consider the human side all the time in any layout'. He goes as far as to suggest 'that a little more humbleness of approach is necessary on the part of some of the designers of residential layouts in particular; there is so often an attempt at the pretentious or geometrical, instead of letting things come more naturally, once you have the programme. Variety, I feel, comes with the programme, with the mixing of various kinds of dwelling, the contrasting blocks of flats with the sweep of a low terrace of houses, the placing of trees, and even the very small buildings for the old folks. None of us like the universal street and the universal house, and they can be avoided if you work out a basic programme of human needs.' Professor Holford referred to the need for experiment in building layout and I feel that is essential. We have to produce a little more audacity and catch some of the spirit of the Victorians in the great building period.' He even explicitly compares Van Eesteren negatively to garden city planners. 'Howard and Unwin and the other pioneers foresaw almost all the points which have come up under discussion. Experiment was one of the things

65

93. Liane Lefaivre, Marlies Boterman, Suzanne Loen, Merel Liedema, 'Een Psychogeografische fietstocht langs de Amsterdamse speelplaatsen van Aldo van Eyck', *Archis*, pp. 129-135, June, 2002.
94. 39a.
95. See memo 425a dated 27 March 1954 where he declares that he is making the playgrounds an integral part of his design of Slotermeer, specifying that they must be the object of requests on the part of the users.
96. NAi, Van Eesteren Archive EEST 1.422. Journal of the Royal Institute of British Architects, 3rd series no. 41, February, 1946, vol. 53. 'Vote of Thanks and Discussion' with Charles Reilly, W.G. Holford.

that Howard emphasized several times in his little book, *Garden Cities of Tomorrow*.'

Another architect, Charles Reilly, is hardly more sparing: 'There is another thing we are in danger of forgetting in modern planning. As human beings we have our private side, and want our homes to ourselves, but we also have a communal side. That communal side has been emphasized all through our history. ... In the great blocks of flats, unless there is a communal room, is there much chance of that? ... Where there is a square, through the children you get to know the other people who live there. Mr Stephenson showed us the plan of Ladbroke Grove area. I know it well because my daughter lives there. The children there can pass out of the private garden into the public garden district without crossing a road, and they soon make friends, and so the people around that garden soon get to know one another.'[97] 'In conclusion, the Garden Cities come up for more praise, this time American examples: Greenbelt Maryland and Buena Vista in Brownville Texas. Interestingly, both are pictured with children playing in playgrounds.'[98]

Van Eesteren must have been shocked by these remarks. One gets the impression they acted as a wake-up call for him; for the very next time we see a plan for Amsterdam West, for the neighbourhood of Slotermeer in 1946 to be precise, the strip housing has been replaced by the kind of courtyard housing favoured by the proponents of the Garden City and Regionalist schools of thought. They are then referred to as 'superblocks'. This marks a 180-degree change of direction in the urban design strategy of Cornelis van Eesteren and the entire City Development Department he directed. And the person who was put in charge of overseeing this change was Jacoba Mulder.

Jacoba Mulder

Jacoba Mulder is far less well known than Aldo van Eyck and Cor van Eesteren. In fact, she was self-effacing to the point that her archive, if it ever existed, cannot be traced in the Municipal Archives of the city she did so much for.[99] She wrote one article in her life. The only traces of her in that archive are some interviews in a teenage girl's magazine, *Margriet*.[100] The only work written about her, by Ellen van Kessel and Froukje Palstra, is 39 pages long.[101]

Jacoba Helena Mulder was born in Breda on 2 March 1900, and entered the Technische Hogeschool Delft (now Delft University of Technology) in 1918. She was one of the first women to graduate from that college, and the first to graduate in the new field of Urban Design. She got a job in 1926 in the municipality of Delft, designing a house for a doctor there, and she worked on the expansion plan for the town. In 1929, she applied to work in Amsterdam at the brand new City Development (*Stadsontwikkeling*) Department of the Public Works Department (*Dienst der Publieke Werken*). Because she was one of the few candidates who had any experience in the field, she got the job. By 1930 she had become the second in command of the City of Amsterdam, under Van Eesteren. They worked together for almost 30 years.[102] He gave her the most important jobs to fill and, upon his retirement, she took his place as director.

Throughout her career, she always tended to go against the grain and to innovate. She was not only highly innovative, however, but she also had both the technical and political skills required to have her innovative ideas realized. Her first big design project in the City Development Department, in the early 1930s, was for the *Amsterdamse Bos*, the Amsterdam Woodland Park, a recreational space. What was unusual about it was that she decided that it ought to follow the English picturesque models favoured by the Garden City designers rather than the stricter, more functional German model. By 1937, the plan was definitive. At 200 acres, it was the biggest green public space ever designed in the Netherlands. The park included a shallow wading pool for children to play in that she designed herself.[103] Later, in the 1950s, she would go back to this idea and introduce the same shallow wading pools in the city of Amsterdam, in the Bellamyplein and Gilbraltarstraat.

Her next project was the Beatrixpark, another recreational space. Berlage had planned a cemetery and a park on the southernmost tip of the city, but the Van Eesteren expansion plan called for a park in another place, Park Zuid. In 1936 she began on the design of the park, which was to become Beatrixpark when it was completed in 1938, named after the newly born Princess Beatrix. The innovation here was that it was the first park that was made exclusively of sand.[104] (Fig.30)

Then came the Amsterdam playgrounds. It was she who got the ball rolling when she walked into work one day in 1947 from her apartment on the Bertelmanplein. 'The idea of the playground layout came to me alone, and I presented it to the Department of Public Works,' she reported in an interview in 1963.[105] 'Things are different for children from 10 and above. They need more space,'

Fig.28
Jacoba Mulder,
Beatrix Park, 1937
(by kind permission
of the Municipal
Archives,
Amsterdam).

67

97. p.113
98. p.111
99. I have been unable to find a trace of her archive in the Municipal Archives of Amsterdam.
100. *Margriet*, no 33, 13 Aug 1960, pp. 23-24. 101 Van Kessel and Palstra, *Ir Jacoba Mulder* (1900-1988), Amsterdam, Stadsdrukkerij, 1994
102. See Van Kessel and Palstra.
103. Cobouw (The Hague), 11.6.1965.
104. ibid
105. Interview with Jacoba Mulder, 'Moeder van de speelplaatsen', *Algemene Dagblad*, 13.4.1963.

she noted. As proof she remarked that 'I saw a little girl from the neighbourhood busy with a shovel digging near a tree. Nice sand came up. She used it for baking tarts with. But then, alas, a dog came by and did his duty and that was the end of that.'[106] This is bottom-up urbanism in the literal sense of the term – a little girl digging in the dirt – the stuff of everyday experience. We are very, indeed, far removed from the grandiose concerns of top-down CIAM planning.

Aldo van Eyck happened to be in the office at the time. He volunteered to design the playground. Van Eesteren agreed. And the playground on the Bertelmanplein, where Mulder lived, was the first of the Amsterdam playgrounds. A neighbour walked by, saw that playground, and wrote to the director of Public Works with a request for another playground, a block or so away. He request was granted. Another passer-by saw it, made a new kind of request. Very soon, requests were coming in fast and furious. That is how the 1000 playgrounds were placed in the city, and how the 6 metres of archives of letters from the citizens, internal memos, and drawings of playgrounds were compiled. Two letters reproduced by Aldo van Eyck are typical. They are signed by all the public servants in the City Development Department who read them.

The subsequent participation politics over the next 20 years are a rare case of democracy in action at an urban level. The letters from the citizens of Amsterdam, requesting playgrounds, or changes in them, speak for themselves (see Appendix 1). Just as remarkable are the memos that circulated within the Department of Public Works in response to these letters (see Appendix 2). Their interstitial and polycentric pattern necessarily arose from the participatory side of the placement of playgrounds – the city embedded playgrounds where the people of Amsterdam felt they should be placed. Each one was made to order, in response to a specific request by a specific citizen or group of citizens for a specific site that had been identified as the potential location for a playground. Some were accepted, and some were not, as we have seen from Van Eesteren's internal correspondence quoted above.

Frankendaal and the PIP Principle:
from Ad-Hoc Procedure to
Clearly Defined Design Tool.

In 1948 comes, arguably, the most important project in connection to playgrounds: Frankendaal. The reason it is important is that this is where the ad-hoc, participatory, interstitial, polycentric procedure that had been responsible for the creation of playgrounds in the traditional inner city of Amsterdam became a design tool for shaping ex-nihilo post-war new towns and housing communities for the first time.

This process also happened in an ad-hoc manner at first. Frankendaal lay in the south of the city and had been planned as a series of strip buildings, based on the pre-war model designed by Van Eesteren in 1935 called Bos en Lommer. The plan for Frankendaal had already been laid out as a series of parallel blocks by the City Development Department under Van Eesteren in 1939. By 1946, however, as we have seen, Van Eesteren had been polemically attacked in London at a meeting of the RIBA. Possibly as a result of the negative reception of the initial strip building project as monotonous and overly rigorous, he gave Mulder the task of analysing the comparative advantages of the facing-L plans, close in shape to the forms that Ludwig Hilberseimer was applying in his regionalist plans.[107] The resulting study, the only one Mulder ever published, appeared in the January 1950 edition of *Publieke Werken*. Her conclusions were in harmony with the Garden City proponents at the RIBA London Meeting. The public space created by the courtyard model, she found, was far superior to the strip housing model. It also provided more spatial variation and increased the amount of light penetrating into the buildings.[108]

Incidentally, from this moment on, Mulder became the advocate of housing built according to the courtyard model, in which two L-shaped buildings are placed opposite one another with an open green space in between. She eventually blended the two, the strip and the courtyard, in her plan of the housing units – Van Eesteren gave her this task while he was involved in larger scale features of the project – in the new city gardens of Amsterdam West, Slotermeer, Sloterdijk, and Geuzeveld.[109]

Back to Frankendaal. By 1948 – two years after the RIBA meeting, Mulder had discarded the original strip buildings in favour of the new plan based on L-shaped blocks. 'It was decided to study the situation again in connection with the altered house-building assignment. The Municipal Housing Department allocated the design of the houses to the *Merkelback en Elling* architectural office. In frequent consultation with the Housing Department, the new plan, now called "Frankendaal", was generated as a part of the Water-graafsmeer project. Figure 1 presents a concise picture of the plan,' she wrote in her article. Frankendaal must have been regarded as an important project in the Urban Development Department for it became something of a showcase housing project – she selected the well-known firm of Merkelbach and Elling to design the duplex

106. Jacoba Mulder, newspaper
107. Ludwig Hilberseimer, *The New City*, Chicago, Theobald, 1944 and Ludwig Hilberseimer, *The New Regional Pattern*, Theobald, 1949
108. Jacoba Mulder, 'Frankendaal', *Publieke Werken*, Jan. 1950, pp.12-14.
109. Van Kessel and Palstra, ibid.

Fig.29
Evolution of the
Frankendaal plan.
The first slab-based
plan is by Van
Eesteren. The last is
by Mulder. Jacoba
Mulder's confi-
guration maintained
the same level of
density as Van
Eesteren's but
provided public
space where his did
not. She used this as
an argument in
general for inter-
locking L-shaped
'superblocks' with a
highly accessible
internal court
structure, enhancing
circulation and
meeting points
between the various
housing units.

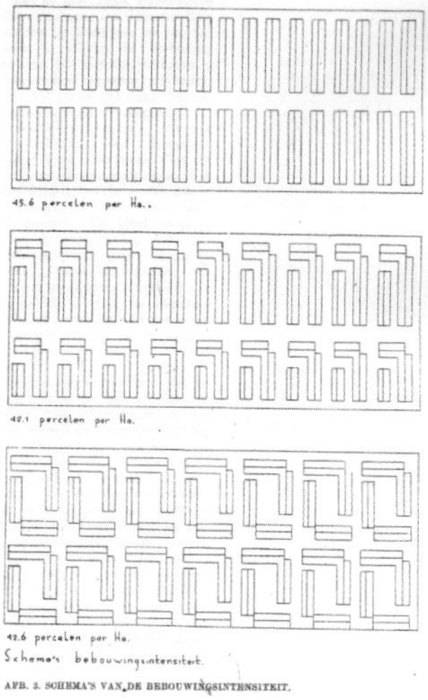

45.6 perceelen per Ha.

46.1 perceelen per Ha.

41.6 perceelen per Ha.
Schema's bebouwingsintensiteit.
AFB. 3. SCHEMA'S VAN DE BEBOUWINGSINTENSITEIT.

70

buildings and the renowned landscape architect Mien Ruys to shape the inner courtyards. The neighbourhood, which included 390 individual houses, acquired the name 'Little Jerusalem'.[110]

Of course, one of the reasons Mulder chose the facing L-shaped housing units for Frankendaal was functional. This kind of unit afforded more light in the interior. As she said herself : 'In connection with the orientation – which is fixed due to the structure of the Watergraafsmeer – the houses around the courtyard have their living rooms facing south-west and south-east, while the access routes lie on the north-west and north-east.'

But somewhere at the back of her mind, even though she did not include them in the illustrations to her article, was the idea that these courtyards could somehow accommodate playgrounds. 'The original design, consisting of strip housing, was replaced by a plan by means of which a form new to Amsterdam, the courtyard, was created. We had sought for a living arrangement that could offer more ambience to the residents than strip housing. This does not mean that Amsterdam has rejected strip housing. It turned out to be possible *to allow* so-called courtyards to arise *in* the space that would otherwise by allocated to sunshine and good incidence of light (editor's italics). The greenery that would otherwise have been needed along the streets is concentrated in this kind of courtyard. The result is that an efficient application of green has been realized for the residents, while it is also possible to design small play areas, sand pits and suchlike for the infants among this greenery.'[111] (Fig.29)

Her article had been published in January. By 27 April 1950, however, it is clear that the idea of the play-grounds had taken shape and discussed with Van Eesteren, for he writes in a correspondence between civil servants, that it is 'logical' that Mien Ruys, who has done the landscape for the Merkelbach housing project 'will also give her vision on the playgrounds'.[112] It is only in 1952 – in an article characteristically not published by her but by Van Eesteren – that she had commissioned Aldo van Eyck to design a series of playgrounds in the inner courtyards.[113] In his article, he retraces the entire evolution of the neighbourhood.

From then on, a participatory, interstitial, polycentered approach to playgrounds, modelled on those of Frankendaal, which had, in turn, been modelled on the playgrounds of the inner city in the years following the Bertelmanplein playground of 1947, became an integral part of the Urban Development's plan for the new garden city developments in Amsterdam West. We

know for example, again from the internal correspondence of the Urban Development Department, that
playgrounds were only inserted in a housing project if
there was a request from the users. (Figs.30-32)

Conclusion

The importance of the Amsterdam playgrounds is that
they provided not just first concept of what the
alternative to the monumental public space conceived
by CIAM might be, but also constituted the first real,
built alternative to it. Amazingly, the playgrounds
combined all the features that would be discussed for
the next twenty years as part of this alternative:
polycentricity, preservation of the urban tissue through
interstitial insertions, and citizen participation. Perhaps
their greatest accomplishment was that they managed to
create a polycentric net of micro 'urban villages' on the
existing functional city, creating a sense of community.
It was still palpable to me sixty years later, at the
opening of the 2003 exhibition that I initiated and
curated at the Stedelijk Museum under the directorship
of Rudi Fuchs on the topic of playgrounds.
The design tool that was concocted in an incremental,
ad-hoc, almost crackpot fashion, through the
interactions of the main actors – Cor van Eesteren,
Jacoba Mulder, Aldo van Eyck, and the citizens of
Amsterdam – is arguably the most successful urban
design tool of the twentieth century, if one is to go by
the wide public acceptance of this design tool.
If they were so successful, the question arises, why has
no one given the Amsterdam playgrounds the attention
they deserve? For all their importance, they have
remained, strangely, even paradoxically, ignored. In
fact, a wave of forgetfulness has engulfed them.
The answer is simple. First, as a factor in urban design
and planning, play was, and still is not taken as
seriously as it should be. And, second, to return to
Denise Scott Brown's expression, we live where 'go-
for-the-jugular' urban practices prevail over bottom-up
concerns such as play and community.
With the evidence presented in the preceding pages, I
hope to have made the case that the design tool based
on the polycentric, interstitial, participatory approach to
playgrounds that emerged from the Amsterdam
playgrounds is worth lifting out of the mists of oblivion
and re-testing as a way of creating public space –
magnets around which micro-urban villages can form –
for both inner-city and peripheral neighbourhoods
today, particularly multi-cultural ones like Oude Westen
and Hoogvliet in Rotterdam.

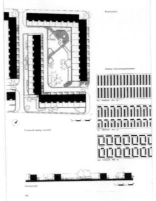

Fig.30
Final plan for
Frankendaal by
Mulder, with Aldo
van Eyck's play-
ground in the centre
of the interlocking
L-shaped apartment
houses and providing
a public space.

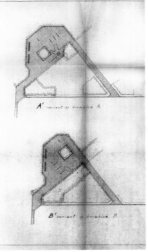

Figs.31,32
Aldo van Eyck
refused to
standardize the play-
grounds. Each one is
a variation on a
theme, 1950
(with kind
permission of the
Municipal Archives,
Amsterdam).

71

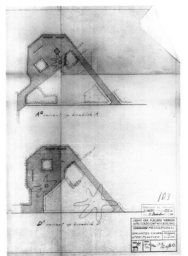

110. The reason for this is unknown to me.
111. Mulder, 1950.
112. 70, 1a.
113 Cornelis van Eesteren, 'Frankendaal: een woonbuurt in de Watergraafsmeer te
Amsterdam', Forum, June/July, 1952, pp. 187-193.

interview by Liane Lefaivre

New York City,
29 September 2004

DAN GRAHAM

Liane Lefaivre: Where do you think we should start in this interview?

Dan Graham: I think we should talk about the first work I did where I discovered that children really liked my work, where I discovered that they were big fans of my work. And also that parents first liked to take photographs of the children playing in my work, but then they decided they also liked to play in my work with the children. I talked about the two audiences, that is, children and parents – the audience inside the work and the audience outside, for public space for the Venice Biennale. Making everything into a showcase. I really liked the idea of a sculpture pavilion, a little like Rietveld's pavilion at Soonsbeck. With Soonsbeck you have small sculptures inside and people inside and outside looking at each other's perceptions. In the Venice Biennale there were two different audiences, children and parents. I knew that many Italians would be there and the acoustic pane piece of glass dividing the two rooms would be soundproof so they could each see each other but not hear each other on the other side. And the idea was to create a lot of gesticulating.

Was it built?

Yes. And it's often shown. In fact it's being shown right now at the van Abbe Museum. It's part of the Herbert Collection. It's a reconstruction of it.

Then what?

Well, then there was a second case. I was showing at the Skulptur exhibition in Munster. There's an 18th-century palace in Munster. The architect's name was Sharon or something like that. I realized than in the *allées*, in the centre of the gardens of this 18th-century palace, there were pavilions and a remaining gazebo. So I did something octagonal. And the roof is tilted at a 15-degree angle. And I put a hole in the centre because I was thinking of Brancusi's work *Hole*. But the hole was very appealing to children, who used to rotate around it. Children liked to put poles there. It became a photo opportunity for children, very kaleidoscopic on the outside and for parents to photograph their children on the inside from the outside. And then, there was a third case. It was when I was invited by Jan Hoet to participate in the Chambre d'Amis in Ghent, Belgium, which was a show during the summer for work inside people's houses or in their gardens or yards. What was interesting was – it was a little political – the taste of the collectors whose influence dominated the museum was nouveau-riche. Not Jean Hoed, whose father was a psychiatrist. So this meant that the interesting people were actually the doctors, an architect, some social workers who were teachers. So what we got to see was the inside of the house. So I decided I should do something for the architect as a client. He had redesigned his back yard and the old house. And he wanted something between the two. So he wanted me to do a little garden pavilion.

But was this a piece expressly for children?

No. What happened was I realized that my piece would be too big if it were a garden piece. It would wreck his architecture. So maybe it wouldn't be good for him professionally. And kids used to play in the area. So I thought of making a neighbourhood children's pavilion instead.

Was that the first one of your sculptures built expressly for children?

Yes. It was the first one expressly for children. It had a pole in the middle and it was very much like two cubes that are rotated at a 45-degree angle, which I'd done before, a little like the Louis Kahn House (note by Liane Lefaivre: he is referring to the Fischer House). There was a movie of it made by French TV. It was a brilliant production.

Then Jeff Wall said 'Why don't we do a children's pavilion together?' The site I chose for the pavilion was right next to La Geode at La Villette. But it was before there was Parc de La Villette. There was a children's mountain there. I redesigned it but without the neo-brutalism. The idea was a children's King of the Mountain. So when boys go to the top they see an oculus. Inside were Jeff Wall's tondos. They could look down into the oculus and see giant images of themselves against the real sky. And their gaze meets the gaze of the parent's inside.

What happened to it?

Nothing. It was never done.

Know any other artists who are interested in play?

Yes, there are other Aries artists, who are now dead. Calder. He was Aries.

Also Mirò was Aries.

What about Fischli and Weiss?

Oh they're the best.

David Weiss and Peter Fischli are both lovers of Rock 'n' Roll. And also both of them play at being normal suburban family men, although they spend so much time travelling around the world. For a certain time other artists were interested in destruction. For example, Roman Singer, another great Swiss artist. The problem with building the Children's Pavilion was that it was designed for a World's Fair situation.

What do you mean World's Fair situation?

It's for international children of the world, and it's a large scale monument. Jeff identifies with the parents looking at the children as gods. I thought it was very influenced by the German painter Otto Runge. He believed children were gods. He was a contemporary of Caspar David Friedrich. He believed that children were gods. It was the romantic idea of children as gods. There was another great artist who dealt with children: Medardo Rosso.

Does childhood play a role in your art?

I was always interested in childhood. I read Sartre when I was 14. In his *Being and Nothingness*, he talks about the formation of the ego when the child sees someone looking at them as that person looks at them as they look at the other person so they mirror each other and give each other an ego. That's the mirror stage. And I think maybe I relate to that. See, I think all art has to do with childhood, childhood situations. My situation was seeing myself as mirrored by somebody else. I have one memory, a horrible memory of when I was asleep inside a car and the windows were rolled up and I couldn't get out of the car. So there's an incredible fragility that small children have but they have a huge egocentric system too. On the other hand without an ego they are lost.

Trapped inside walls of glass, seeing but not being seen. So your work is really shaped by this childhood experience?

Well, it's basically about phenomenology. Minimal art was about an object. And what I was interested in was the creation of the spectator involved in perception. I think I got this partly from Michael Snow. And I was particularly interested that Nauman used the body. I have involved myself as a spectator watching a performance of his.

How do you think your art relates to children?

My art was more for children though than about children. See, in 'Children's Pavilion', I liked the fact that boys liked to be king of the mountain. And also when they see themselves,

73

they see themselves as giants. In the concave mirror against the sky, they're giants. And they see the parents inside looking up very small. And almost insignificant. And of course inside there's a convex mirror, there's a fish-eye lens and people can see their gazes superimposed on the gazes of the children. And in the Dia Foundation piece, boys on the inside of the circular interior element see themselves as giants but, on the other side, women see themselves as very thin on the fish-eye lens part. The boys like to see themselves as giants and the girls and grown women as slender figures. So I'm playing with people's expectations. Also what I wanted to do in my curved things is to move toward baroque. I started that some time ago in Munich. Munich rococo was very important to me.

You are, in other words, one of the artists today who are most concerned with childhood and play.

Yes. My interest in children was a reaction to the art of the late '80s, when everything was neo-expressionist, European expressionist. My other interest in children is that not only were children big fans of my work, but I realized that the modern museums need educational areas where children can have access to computers and videos as educational sources. For my Dia piece I actually conceived a coffee bar where they would have cartoons for children. The cylinder of the DIA piece was even surrounded with a rubber ground so kids could play there without getting hurt.

Your Dia piece was conceived as another children's pavilion?

The idea was for the art piece to be used by children. So kids could play in it. It was meant for parents and children. Does anyone know that? I don't know.

interview by Liane Lefaivre

Vienna, MAK Café,
4 November 2004

ERWIN WURM

Liane Lefaivre: Are you interested in play?

Erwin Wurm: Yes very much, a big part of my work is about playing. There are two kinds of playing, the one is to play on your own yourself and then to play with someone else. I am very much about playing with someone else, about this seduction thing.

So, all your art is about playing with someone, engaging them?

A big part is, a very big part.

Why is this? Were you influenced by other artists?

Yes, maybe by the seventies or so, maybe also by Dada. Humour is like reality seen from another perspective, from a strange and funny perspective. For example, when you think about it, becoming fat is a tragedy. Making it funny makes it fun. And fun seduces you into come closer, into being more

intimate. **And one day I realized I liked this very much. And from that point on, I always wanted to create something where people reacted first by thinking 'how funny' but then by realizing: Oh, this is weird or strange or This is a philosophical statement. But the way to engage people is always to have them think 'how funny' first. I also believe that humour is a way of being able to love more about myself and about other things.**

Are you interested in play in your art because you think it touches people more? It is a way of being in touch with people?

Absolutely.

Does this have anything to do with the easy?

One way of getting people's attention is to make things simple. Simple doesn't mean stupid. Simple can mean

stupid, **of course, but it can also mean clear, or light. Saying things about, for example, political incorrectness, terrorism and other really important, serious things in a funny way is just another way of speaking about them.**

You can make funny art about terrorism?

Yes. I made a series that is called 'instructions on how to be political incorrect'. Part of it consists of two images. The first is called Looking for a Bomb. In it, you see a man putting his hand in the pants of another man who has something in his crotch visible in the bulge of his trousers. And then you see the same image again, but this time with a girl who has her hand in his pants. This photograph is also called Looking for a Bomb. Of course, in the beginning it is

**funny, but then immediately
you realize, on second
thoughts, that it is not funny. I
deal with the same political
issues most artists today are
dealing with, just the register is
different.**

What about Huizinga's *Homo
Ludens*? He argues that play is
really the basis of civilization.

**Absolutely. I mean, that is
play. Absolutely. Sadness is
always presented as having
imposing cultural importance
and I think it is wrong, it is
just wrong. Playfulness should
be taken far more seriously.**

interview by Liane Lefaivre

Palais de Tokyo, Paris,
25 October 2004

JEROME SANS

Liane Lefaivre: Of all the Museum directors, I thought I would ask you about what you thought about play. Was I mistaken?

Jerome Sans.: You are the only person who can know this. Second question!

Does playfulness appeal to you as a concept?

Absolutely. I adore play. I think that play is at the centre of life. Life is a permanent game. And we are part of it. That's why, indeed, it interests me very much.

Is this why you wrote a 'Praise of the Absurd'? Is there more to the absurd than just play for the sake of play? Is there something more profound about it?

Absolutely.

What is it that makes the absurd so significant?

I would say that through the absurd you can make profound things come to the surface. The absurd is a way, a kind of operational means, of speaking about things that are essential. If you talk about them in a brutal way, often it doesn't work. Through the absurd you have a better way for things to get by, to come out into the open, for ideas to advance, for people to be confronted with reality.

This is the case with the art of Erwin Wurm for instance?

Yes, he's a good example. His work in general approaches life in a pretty absurd way, in a way that is quite reduced, quite minimal, quite simple. His 'One minute sculptures' are a sort of extraordinarily ironical comment on performance art, on the history of contemporary art, and put us in situations that are very absurd, and permanently. How to make a body stand, how to play with an object, improbable situations or grotesque, where all of a sudden, for an instant, the object becomes innovated. And I think this is contemporary art, it's things that only exist for a brief moment. All of a sudden we decide that a certain thing becomes a work of art. It can last 15 seconds, 2 hours, a little more. But every time it's a question of a particular temporality: how do we know how long a work you are looking at will be a work of art? 5 seconds? A minute? 2 hours? 15 days? 30 years? Nothing is granted a priori. You are left to your own devices. You have to define its temporality for yourself. It's strange. Think of it. Temporality is one of those rare things that has no absolute duration, no validity. Every thing – a newspaper, a film, a disk – has a temporality.

77

Art is one of the rare things that foil the notion of temporality. It creates a timeless time. All you have to do is look at the inflation of video artists that create videos that are in a never-ending loop. They are, curiously, films that have no beginning, no middle and no end.

Perhaps Fatness is a comment on the over-inflated bubble of the late 1990s.

Of course. This is a period where everything is on the verge of exploding. There is so much information that we are ready to burst. One has to spend at least two hours per week in a gym in order to loose all these calories. And speaking of Wurmian inflation, I am personally involved in it since he made a 'Jerome Fat'. Very fat. The absurdity of this piece is extraordinary. All the media, no matter what they are, are always showing contemporary man to be more dynamic, to be more efficient, to be more handsome, to be more fantastic, to be an incredible aesthete. And for women to have no faults, with everything under control, like food, someone who is capable of loosing weight before the summer, who knows how to be magnificent on the beach. Erwin Wurm is the opposite. He turns all this upside down. Everyone produces Lite products, he produces Fat products. How in one week to double your weight. This is exactly the opposite of what the people in the society of consumption try to make us believe is good. Their message is always that we can constantly be better, to resemble the canon presented in magazines or films where super heroes are ever more

beautiful and efficient. Therefore I believe his work is important in this sense.

Erwin Wurm is one of the most playful artists today, I suppose. He is very playful, and he plays a lot, of course. He plays with the system, with the means of inverting the classical situation, bringing you, the spectator, into grotesque positions where we become the voyeur of us, ourselves.

And you as a museum director, do you play too?

Of course. Everyday is a game, a multiple game. You play everyday with the institution. You put yourself at risk, in danger. Permanently. Concerning budgetary matters, economical ones, your public follows you constantly, it's like being on stage every single night. Every director of every institution is a player. There are big players. Then there are players that are funny, and ones that are less funny. Some are more timid. Others confront the system and the rules of the game. The thing about art is that it's a game without rules. Because the rules of art are constantly being reinvented. It would seem that this is the law of art. The idea of the game is particularly interesting because you are usually the maker of the rules of your own game. And there are very few areas of life where you can invent the rules of the game yourself. In all the places of contemporary society, I believe art is one of the rare places where you can invent and impose your own rules and say which ones are good.

So all art is play?

The artist is someone who constantly invents his or her

own rules. Take any worker in today's world. He or she is not the one who invents the rules of the game. You are born within a system which imposes its own rules. The artist is one of the rare people who is still able to say 'je' (I), who is able to exist today as a 'je'. Normally, this is the very principle of the artist. Fortunately! When art takes itself seriously, that's serious! It's always like that. When you start taking yourself seriously, it's serious. You have to constantly question yourself. Life is a game, of course. It's a permanent game. It can be euphoric, dramatic, positive. And negative.

Games can be negative?

Yes. Sometimes. You can lose at a game. But you also can lose yourself in a game. In a game you can drown yourself. I think that all artists are players. They play their games in relation to the public. To be an artist is to play, above all, from a social point of view, and to say: Wait a minute, I am artist, I live outside society, I live differently. To be an artist is not an easy thing. In the capitalist world we live in, being an artist is a totally incredible stance to take. Art is the last bastion where you can still say 'je'. J-E and J-E-U (he spells out the words 'je' and 'jeu' which are pronounced the same in French. This is a play on words).

You mean 'je' equals 'jeu'?

Of course. Didn't this ever occur to you? It's obvious.

Has it always been like this?

Of course. That is why artists are so still fascinating today. Whatever your place is in society, you exist only as part of a group. The artist is

someone that can exist on his
or her own.

What did you train in?

Nothing. I studied nothing. My
studies were made, in fact, as
part of a 'jeu', by confronting
artists. I learned everything I
know by visiting artists'
studios. In France and abroad.
By speaking with them. I was
like Plato or Socrates. I went
into the City. I walked the City.
I talked with people. Life
consisted in learning by talking
with people. True knowledge is
the knowledge of how to play.

And is architecture a game too?

Obviously. All the elements are
there. A game is complete. A
game is not just a few things
laid out on a table. You have to
have a certain element, there
has to be a certain cohesion to
the game. Otherwise it's
counterfeit. It's not natural.
Everything must be coherent
in a game.

Are there artists who are more
playful than others?

79

No. There are no 'heroes of
playfulness'. All art is a game.

DÖLL

PLAY NETWORKS FOR ROTTERDAM

In the historical part of this study, Liane Lefaivre presents the PIP model. This stands for Participation, Interstitial (the in-between) and Polycentric (network). The model is based on the approach that was the foundation of the post-war playgrounds designed by Van Eyck and others in the old inner city and the urban expansions of Amsterdam, the *Westelijke Tuinsteden* (Western Garden Cities). Participation refers to the interactive processes between residents and the municipality within which the play areas came about: the play areas were realized at the moment the residents informed the local authorities of their need for them. Another strong point of the play areas is the degree in which they adjust themselves to the weave of the urban development, called 'interstitial' by Lefaivre. The play areas are embedded naturally which provides great quality of use and social control. Together these play areas form a 'polycentric' network, a web of many small play areas. The great density of small play areas mean children can conquer public places step by step and that playing becomes an integral part of the neighbourhood.

The practical study tests the extent to which this model, as an urban strategy for a play network, can offer a solution to a present-day requirement.

The timing for a new vision of play in the city could not be better. Attention to the playing child has increased greatly in the Netherlands in the past few years. The active lobby of foundations that devote effort to stimulating children's play (such as Jantje Beton in the Netherlands and the Child-friendly Cities network internationally) is beginning to bear fruit. The exponential increase of overweight children (more than 17% in the Netherlands)[1] has worked as a catalyst. Politicians are becoming aware of the social costs involved and are starting to prioritize the promotion of physical exercise. The idea prevails that children are less active due to the advent of the TV and the computer. The TNO study entitled *Kinderen in prioriteitswijken* (Children in Priority Neighbourhoods, 2005) refutes this assumption by demonstrating that the primary cause of physical inactivity is the lack of (suitable) outdoor playing areas. Having studied a sample of over twelve hundred children from underprivileged neighbourhoods in the Netherlands (among whom around 30% are overweight), TNO concluded that children in urban quarters with more greenery, low-rise buildings, sports fields and collective parking places are much more active than children in urban quarters where the traffic flows are more intense and the streets more polluted. Another recent study, *Kinderen in Tel* [2] (Dutch Kids Count), on the lifestyle of children in the Netherlands, shows that large cities in particular (but not exclusively) score poorly as a living environment for children to grow up in. The outcome of these and other studies have resulted in political intervention at national level.[3]

The increasing attention aimed at improving public space not only stems from the need to stimulate play and movement among children. In the integration debate, play space has also become a point of order. At the end of 2005, the Council for Social Development (in Dutch: RMO) published the report entitled *Niet langer met de ruggen tegen elkaar* (No Longer Back to Back), which was commissioned by the Ministry of Immigration and Integration. This report provides a practical translation of the concept of 'inter-ethnic bonding'. This inter-ethnic bonding is part of the new Dutch model for integration policy that the RMO established earlier in 2005.[4] Inter-ethnic bonding refers to the genesis of social relationships between groups consisting of different nationalities. The RMO defines three means of reinforcing these connections: the elimination of socio-economic arrears, the establishment of sustainable and ongoing integration projects, and the stimulation of public familiarity. To stimulate public familiarity, the RMO advocates the creation of spontaneous meeting places in public space. The location and layout of these places should bring people together on the basis of shared interests, such as parenthood. The playground is a public area *par excellence* that promotes interaction between parents and other people of different backgrounds.

Thus, every reason to prioritize the installation of playgrounds. So far, the focal point seems to be of a quantitative nature. More playgrounds, however, do not necessarily mean more quality play space. The level of ambition in terms of quality is generally rather low, and little money is available for designing and realizing playgrounds that live up to their potential as community-enhancing public space. Liane Lefaivre's PIP model supplies a potentially interesting design method to realize qualitative output in the field of urban playground design. To test the applicability of the PIP model in a present-day context, we research it as a design strategy for Oude Westen and Hoogvliet, two spatially and socially different neighbourhoods in Rotterdam.

The discussion on the identity of the city and the place of the child in it is topical in Rotterdam. In a comparison among almost five hundred Dutch municipalities, Rotterdam scores the worst in terms of child-friendliness.[5] Of the 138,000 children who live in Rotterdam[6] more than two thirds live in deprived neighbourhoods, and one third of the children come from underprivileged families. With an index of

62 children per hectare of playing area, Rotterdam does not score worse than other large Dutch municipalities such as Amsterdam, Utrecht, and The Hague. Nevertheless, the perception of Rotterdam is everything but child-friendly. The traffic machine leaves its mark on Rotterdam to a greater extent than on other cities. During the post-war reconstruction that followed the devastation of WWII, Rotterdam ruthlessly transformed into a modern city in which cars were prioritized as users of public space.

With respect to inter-ethnic bonding, the debate in Rotterdam is rather fierce. With 125 spoken languages and an ever-expanding number of immigrants or people of direct immigrant descent (at this moment over 40% of the total population) defining a multicultural society is a prime concern for the politicians. Economic en socio-cultural backlogs seem to be concentrated in specific areas in Rotterdam. They are accumulating into unsafe and downward-spiralling situations. That is why the municipal authorities are advocating a neighbourhood-oriented approach to deal with these problems. Various bodies are co-operating to tackle spatial and social problems. The test locations for the PIP model, the Oude Westen and Hoogvliet (Meeuwenplaat) are two Rotterdam neighbourhoods that are being revamped. They exemplify typical Dutch inner-city and post-war quarters. In both cases, the construction of a network of play spaces offers a solution to the above-mentioned issues: they provide safe play areas for children and, as low-threshold meeting places, promote a stronger sense of community within and across ethnicities.

81

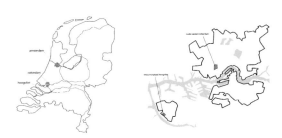

Case studies on location:
Oude Westen and Meeuwenplaat, Rotterdam

ROTTERDAM AS TESTING GROUND

OUDE WESTEN

The nineteenth-century neighbourhood Oude Westen is a typical Dutch inner-city quarter. Situated at the heart of Rotterdam, and wedged between busy shopping streets and at a stone's throw from the central Station, it accommodates 10,000 people. With around 25% of the residents under 19 years of age, Oude Westen is the quarter with by far the most children compared to other neighbourhoods in the city centre.[7] It is a real immigrant neighbourhood. Three quarters of the population are immigrants – with Turkish, Moroccan, and Surinamese roots in particular. In Dutch terms, Oude Westen is a poor area. In 2000, one third of the residents lived under the official poverty line[8] and a large number of families currently depend on charity food packages. Only 8% of the housing stock of the largely pre-war quarter is owner-occupied.[9] Relative poverty, crime, and insecurity are often interrelated. The liveability is also under pressure in Oude Westen. Despite considerable improvements over the past few years, the neighbourhood still scores poorly, with a count of 3.5 on the Rotterdam security index.[10] Crime is concentrated in and around the shops and catering establishments along the shopping streets. The presence of vagrants and junkies, who have been forced out of former drugs locations now enter the neighbourhood via the adjoining shopping street, contributing to a sense of insecurity.

Of course, figures do not tell the whole truth. Oude Westen is not a ghetto, but rather a lively 'working-class' quarter with strong social cohesion that is valued by many as a pleasant living environment. A striking phenomenon worth mentioning is the presence of a great number of instances in the neighbourhood. The Wenk (Welfare and Child) Foundation, Aktiegroep Oude Westen, the Odeon community centre, the Play-o-theque, and the Turkish Participation Platform are just a few examples. These instances and the people who work there form a network that, as a separate social layer in Oude Westen, tackles the problems and brings residents of different backgrounds together.

Morphology

The rich history of Oude Westen is captured in its layered structure. Its hidden character is the legacy of a number of interventions that have taken place in the lee of Rotterdam's city centre in the course of centuries. The Westersingel, which marks the eastern boundary of the neighbourhood, is a part of city architect Rose's renowned Singel Plan dating from the end of the nineteenth century. The aim of this plan was to expand the city to accommodate the prosperous middle classes. The area fell into the hands of speculators who built working-class houses on the narrow parcels between the polder ditches, thus creating the typical pattern of long

1974

2006

Historical overview of Oude Westen: Josephstraat in 1952, billboard by the *Oude Westen Action Group* in the 1970s; changes in the urban blueprint under the influence of the Stadsvernieuwing (urban renewal).

84

Rotterdam, 2006
Quarter: Oude Westen

	Oude Westen	Rotterdam
Total number of residents	9,954	596,597 (2005)
% population 0 to four years old	6.1	5.9
% population 5 to 9 years old	5.6	5.5
% population 10 to 14 years old	5.5	5.6
% population 15 to 19 years old	7.4	6
% of immigrant descent	73.4	46
% of Dutch descent	26.6	54
Total number of houses	4,422	285,933
% of rented houses	90	74
% owner-occupied houses	9	25
Safety index score	2.7	6.6

Source: Municipal Registry (GBA)

north-south streets without squares or parks. The houses were poorly founded and the area was not connected to the city sewerage or city lighting. However, Oude Westen became a popular residential quarter due to the growing population pressure in the old centre. The 1930s witnessed the construction of the traffic arteries the Gravendijkwal and the Mathenesserlaan, under the management of city architect De Jongh. Oude Westen obtained a formal east and southern boundary. The northern boundary that had been formed by the old zoological garden has remained indeterminate since the WWII bombing. The formal boundaries gradually became so conspicuous that the neighbourhood itself seemed invisible. Nevertheless, the vitality of the neighbourhood, with its many shops, bars and small companies, was known throughout Rotterdam. Two old connections that traverse Oude Westen, the West-kruiskade and the Oude Binnenweg, were forcibly adopted into the plans as trunk roads. These streets, which divide Oude Westen into three independently functioning sections, still play a major role in the daily life of the neighbourhood as a shopping area and meeting place.

Social shifts and urban renewal
After the Second World War, several plans were developed to demolish Oude Westen and to integrate the area in the new, modern city centre. The inner city was considered to be no longer suitable for living functions. Despite the fact that the plans were never implemented, the persistent threat of demolition had a great influence on the neighbourhood. There was little investment in the houses and infrastructure. Many residents, especially the workers, moved to the new suburbs, so that the small workplaces disappeared. Immigrant workers and students took their place. The neighbour-hood quickly transformed from a homogeneous working-class neighbourhood into a culturally diverse quarter. In the 1970s, various housing associations acquired ownership of the majority of the houses. At the same time, ideas on the city changed again. There was no longer an attempt to edge the living function out of the city. Instead, a mixture of functions had become the ideal configuration. This insight was not only current in the realm of designers and policy-makers, but the threatening demolition plans and neglect of the neighbourhood also moved the residents to take action. This resulted in the foundation of the 'Aktiegroep Oude Westen' (Action Committee for Oude Westen), which has had great influence on local politics right up to the present day. Persuaded by the passionate actions undertaken by the residents, the policy-makers realized that the social, cultural and spatial structure ought to be respected in all urban revitalization projects. 'Building for the neighbourhood' became the slogan of a new policy called 'Stadsvernieuwing' (urban renewal). The aim was to alleviate the poverty and stem the flight to the suburbs.[11] Oude Westen was the first integral urban renewal project in the Netherlands. In the period from 1973 to 1993, work was performed on urban regeneration, with the aim of improving the physical and social structure of the neighbourhood. The Municipality, designers and residents collaborated intensely, with the existing urban fabric of Oude Westen forming the point of departure. At the same time, the characteristic long narrow streets and the closed, shallow building blocks represented the greatest obstacle. It was decided to create space without corroding the structure. Demolishing parts of the building blocks created squares. Lateral breaches from west to east created space and made it possible to meander through the neighbourhood. The problem with parking was partly solved by building semi-sunken car parks under the inner courts. Building blocks were united, which ensured more incidence of light and space in the inner courts, and enabled dual ground use, as was the case with the semi-sunken car parks with gardens and play areas above them.

At this moment, Oude Westen is going through a new phase of intensive restructuring, a step impelled by the need to enhance the quality of the neighbourhood and to make it safer. Owner-occupied houses will replace a considerable part of the cheaper houses, and the public space will be upgraded.

85

ROTTERDAM AS TESTING GROUND

HOOGVLIET

Hoogvliet is one of the most famous post-war neighbourhoods in the Netherlands. It lies to the south-west of Rotterdam, wedged between the Nieuwe and the Oude Maas on the south-west side, and the motorway with petrochemical industry (Pernis) on the north side. We focused on one particular neighbourhood of Hoogvliet, Meeuwenplaat. Meeuwenplaat is a part of Lotte Stam-Beese's blueprint for Hoogvliet. The neighbourhood has a population of approximately 4,300 people. They mostly live in rented flats in the social sector. The fact that 43% of the residents are older than 55 years is remarkable; the Rotterdam average is 24% for this age group.[12] Most houses were built in the 1960s in accordance with the idea of the New Towns, which aimed at providing light, air and space. The combination of high-density building with the retention of the human scale was achieved by grouping housing strips of various heights around communal green courts. These units were repeated in regular patterns. Thus the characteristic stamp structure of Dutch post-war plans was created.

Influenced by changing architectural insights and partly due to its isolated position in relation to Rotterdam, the Meeuwenplaat gradually degenerated.

The neighbourhood is now undergoing radical and intensive restructuring. The first plans have already been realized and considerable demolition has taken place. At the time of writing, around 30% of the houses were unoccupied. To maintain an impression of occupancy, all the curtains of the empty houses are kept closed. But anyone walking through the Meeuwenplaat immediately feels the emptiness of the neighbourhood. The curtains may fool the eye but not the mind. The streets look desolate. Apart from the school, there are few social institutions. Their cohesive power in the social fabric is tangibly lacking. The restructuring phase has had an effect on the appreciation of the residents for the neighbourhood. The *Onderzoek op Maat* office (Custom-made Survey) charted the opinion of the Hoogvliet residents in 2003. Their survey indicated that half of the residents believed that the neighbourhood had declined and that they felt insecure in their own neighbourhood.

One neighbourhood, three zones
The Meeuwenplaat is divided into three spatially and socially separate zones. The northern zone borders on the Oedevlietse Park and consists of expansively laid-out structures. Most flats have storage areas and a porch entrance on the ground floor. Several apartments on the ground floor have private gardens that border on the public green areas. This zone was the last one to be built the Meeuwenplaat. It is the only area that accommodates students and is the area where most

Age categories	percentage of residents
0-5 years	8%
6-12 years	9%
13-17 years	5%
Total 0-17	**22%**
18-24 years	8%
25-29 years	13%
30-34 years	11%
35-39 years	7%
40-44 years	4%
45-49 years	4%
50-54 years	9%
Total 18-54	**56%**
55-59 years	8%
60-64 years	7%
65-74 years	6%
75+ years	2%
Total 55+	**23%**

Ethnic origins

Dutch descent	60%
Immigrant descent	40%

Source of age data: Vestia, Rotterdam
Source of ethnic origins: Liveability monitor2003,
Bureau onderzoek op Maat

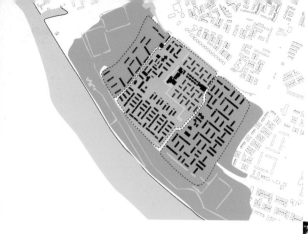

In spatial and social terms, Meeuwenplaat (Hoogvliet) is divided into three zones.
pink: north zone, orange: central zone, green: south zone.

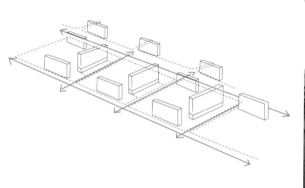

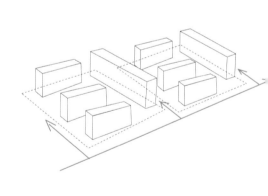

Impression of the north zone (top)
Impression of the central zone (bottom)
Impression of the south zone (right)

people live who have completed higher education and whose chief occupation is paid employment.[10]

This zone also differs from the others in appearance. For a long time it was regarded the most insecure area in the neighbourhood. Drugs nuisance and crime prevailed. Accordingly, this was the area where the restructuring was first implemented. This zone will be a building site in the coming few years.

The central zone is primarily made up of 'garden patterns' that consist of two-storey single-family homes with a front and back garden. Publicly-accessible garden paths separate the back gardens from one another. This area is generally populated by people aged forty and older.[10] The eastern part of the central zone is the oldest part of the neighbourhood. Two thirds of the residents are aged 55 years and older. Gardening has become a real popular art in many of the streets. A micro-society has evolved here. People regularly meet to chat and try to outdo one another in the cultivation of their gardens.

The southern zone is made up of patterns with the characteristic post-war comb structure. These patterns consist of a long apartment block with three smaller blocks attached at right angles. The blocks consist of four layers with storage areas on the ground floor. Relatively many families live here, partly due to the proximity of the school complex. Restructuring will also intensively affect this part in the coming years. The current patterned structure will largely be replaced by single-family homes with private gardens.

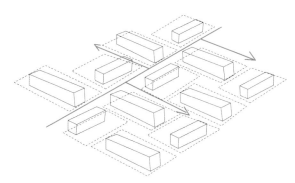

Morphology

The turbulent genesis of Hoogvliet is legible in its architectural structure. Hoogvliet is traditionally a ribbon village on a polder dike near the Oude Maas river. The population lived from agriculture and salmon fishing. The Oude Maas was once connected to the tidal water known as the Hoogvlietse Gat. The area around the Ruigeplaatbos is still a tidal area with unique flora and fauna. The round forms of Hoogvliet can be traced back to the original circular accretion polders on which new outer layers of accretion gradually accumulated.[13] With a few decades from 1951 onward, Hoogvliet grew from an agrarian and fishing village into a modern satellite suburb. The cause was the strong post-war growth of the harbours and industry (including the settlement of Shell in the 1940s) in the nearby area, generating a need for accommodation for the workers.[14] At the end of the forties, Hoogvliet was planned as a modern New Town that would contain around 18,000 houses for 60,000 residents. It was built in seven sections each containing around 3000 houses, in line with the principle of the English neighbourhoods that nestle along radials equidistant from the city centre. Full

Historical map of Hoogvliet: the round forms of the original
'circular accretion polders' are still recognizable in the
present-day structure of Hoogvliet.

of optimism, construction started in Nieuw Engeland, Westpunt, Zalmplaat, and Meeuwenplaat. H.C. Milius, L. Stam-Beese, H. Maaskant, Van Tijen and H. Bakker were responsible for the modernist urban planning and architecture. The construction of the zones progressed rapidly, and a modern city centre steadily replaced the old dike village. Old traces of the landscape and the ribbon village vanished almost completely. Only the seventeenth-century village church in the city centre and the adjoining dike road remained intact. Scarcely twenty years later, construction stagnated under the influence of changing ideals. The idea of the self-sufficient satellite city was overtaken by new ideas in which monotonous high-density construction and living in the vicinity of heavy industry were regarded as undesirable.[15] Twenty years after Rotterdam Municipal Council had sanctioned Hoogvliet as a satellite city, a number of councillors realized that a spatial planning blunder had occurred and they refused to co-operate in the further development of Hoogvliet. Instead of the planned 60,000 residents, Hoogvliet had 36,000 at that time.[12] The decision was taken to build the remaining sections in lower-density construction and the metro railway line was not extended to the centre. This half-hearted solution ensured that Hoogvliet became a city with two faces. On the one hand, there was the strict hierarchy of the monotonous modernist satellite city, on the other, it was a suburban garden city.[13] As a consequence, the facilities, such as public transport and shops, could not function properly. These two faces of Hoogvliet can both be found in the Meeuwenplaat. There is a part with high-rise construction, with four-storey porch-entrance apartment blocks, and a part with single-family homes.

Downwards spiral and restructuring
Employment dropped in the seventies and eighties due to the oil crisis and increasing automation in industry. The closure of the Shell refinery on Curaçao also had an impact. As a consequence, a relatively large group of Antilleans with little future prospects arrived in Hoogvliet hoping to find employment in one of the factories in the adjoining Pernis. Financial capacity diminished, shopping centres did little business and were eventually boarded up. The imago of Hoogvliet worsened. The restructuring of Hoogvliet began in the early nineties. It was typified by the unconventional approach Known as WiMBY!, *Welcome in My Backyard*, a new approach introduced under the guidance of the art historians Van Stiphout and Provoost. WIMBY! is a long-term programme of co-operative projects various fields, including architecture, urban design, and visual art. The working method is characterized by the use and reinforcement of the existing social and physical qualities if Hoogvliet as the basis for renewal.[16]

1 Source: Alterra, 2006 (not yet published)
2 *Databoek Kinderen in Tel*, Verwey-Jonker Institute (2006). The data book is the Dutch variant of the American *Kids Count*. The Verwey-Jonker Institute is an independent social research organization.
3 In a letter dated 14 April 2006, Minister Dekker of Housing, Spatial Planning and the Environment summoned the Municipal Council to ensure that there was sufficient playing area, with 3% of the spatial planning as guideline.
4 *Eenheid, verscheidenheid en binding. Over concentratie en integratie van minderheden in Nederland* (Unity, Variety, and Bonding. On concentration and integration of minorities in the Netherlands), Raad voor Maatschappelijke Ontwikkeling (2005).
5 *Databoek kinderen in tel*, Verwey – Jonker Institute (2006)
6 *Kerncijfers Rotterdam 2005* (Indicators for Rotterdam), Centraal Bureau voor de Statistiek, CBS (Centre for Research and Statistics), Municipality of Rotterdam
7 Central Research Institute Rotterdam
8 € 9,435 on an annual basis, Centraal Bureau voor de Statistiek (CBS)
9 The Rotterdam average is 23% (Central Research Institute Rotterdam).
10 The safety index gives a score on the basis of various data, including the registration of crime, residents' evaluation, and the average income. The scores range from 1 (unsafe) to 10 (safe) for the liveability in the entire city and all the neighbourhoods. Source: www.rotterdamveilig.nl, date of visit, May 2006.
11 Van der Gaag, S. et al. (ed.), *Oude Westen, laboratorium van de stadsvernieuwing* (Laboratory of Urban Renewal), Rotterdam (010 publishers) 1993.
12 *Leefbaarheidsmonitor 2003* (Liveability Monitor), Bureau op Maat (2003).
13 Oerlemans, H., *Landschappen in Zuid-Holland*, The Hague (SDU publishers) 1992
14 Wolters, R, Hoogvliet, *Woonstad tussen Shell en Oude Maas*, Zaltbommel (European Library) 2000
15 Provoost, M. et al., *WiMBY, Welcome into my backyard!*, Rotterdam (NAI publishers) 2000.
16 Source: www.wimby.nl, consulted in August 2006

PLAY
SPACE

OUDE
WESTEN

Before testing the PIP model, we inventoried the quantitative and qualitative play potential, or 'playability', for all age groups, of the available outdoor space in Oude Westen and Meeuwenplaat. To gain a structured insight in the play area, each place has been labelled, where the labels indicate the physical features (materials and accessibility), the target group (intended age category), and the play facilities of every place. Subsequently, characterizing play areas have been assigned typological forms in reference to both of these neighbourhoods.

In Oude Westen, most open squares have been laid out as play areas. During the urban renewals that took place between 1973 and 1993, the scarce outdoor space was transformed into a living room and meeting place for all residents of the neighbourhood. Almost every open area of any size – mostly created by the demolition of building blocks – was laid out with a few trees and benches and some playing equipment. In total, we counted 26,000 m2 of outdoor playing space, which amounts to 10m2 for each child. According to some common rules of thumb, this ought to be sufficient. It is all the more remarkable that a number of playgrounds give a rundown impression. Investigation showed that vandalism was not the cause. The equipment is simply overused, and consequently does not fulfil its estimated lifespan. This is a direct result of the fact that the housing consists mainly of apartments and the children are dependent on public facilities if they want to play. In the research period, the play areas in Oude Westen were characterized by their great uniformity in terms of design and amenities. Instead of being small oases in the urban fabric, the stony layout of the squares reflect the closed character of the surroundings. The inner courts are exceptional playing areas. These semi-public areas have been made playable to a certain extent and represent safe places for younger children in particular. The neighbourhood park is the only green park in the vicinity. With grassy fields, a children's farm, community garden and benches, it provides facilities for all age groups. However, the eccentric situation in the neighbourhood restricts accessibility and thus the user quality.

Certain groups seem to have been forgotten when the playing areas were laid out. Most squares are too large and too busy for the youngest children. For adults, there is too little space to sit and relax and to be involved in the dynamics of the surroundings at the same time. The facilities for young people aged from 13 to 18 years are also restricted. Many spots are laid out for children but are claimed by adolescents out of pure necessity. Community workers compensate the lack of facilities by organizing sport and play activities. Representatives of the squares take good care of the play areas and make sure the various groups don't get in one another's way. The acute need for playing space accentuates the lack of facilities at many places in Oude Westen.

Analysis of play space in Oude Westen.
Physical features (orange = hard landscaped, green = green, black dashed = traffic-free streets) and play facilities (pink labels).

93

Play typologies in Oude Westen

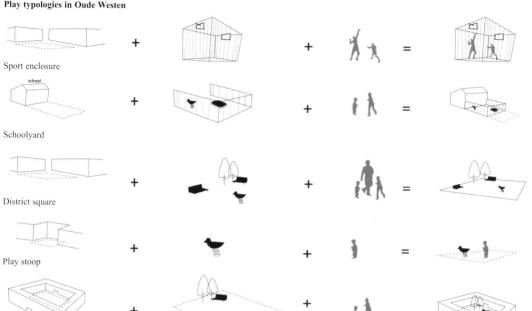

Sport enclosure

Schoolyard

District square

Play stoop

Inner court

District park

The play typologies in Oude Westen reflect their urban context with mostly hard landscaped facilities. The inner courts offer the safest play space for young children and gardens for the adults.

Play typologies in Hoogvliet

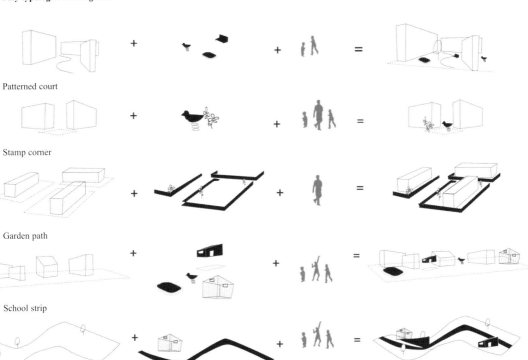

Patterned court

Stamp corner

Garden path

School strip

Green swathe

The play structure in Meeuwenplaat is defined more by spaces than by places, with a small variety in play facilities, for the most part intended for young children.

PLAY
SPACE

At first sight, the green Meeuwenplaat resembles a large playground as a whole. There is a total of 100,000 m2 of potential playing area, mainly in the form of expansive green fields in which play equipment has been placed here and there. This means that each child up to the age of 19 years has around 100 m2 of play area at his or her disposal. The Oedevlietse Park and the park along the shores of the Maas have not been taken into account. Despite this abundance of space, one can question the play potential of the Meeuwenplaat. First of all, the public (playing) area is primarily laid out as monotonous visual greenery. In the communal inner courts, the central green swathe and the smaller green strips accommodate the basic (play) functions.

The identical layout does not do justice to this potential. The playgrounds are spaces instead of places. This does not make them interesting play locations. The few places that have been genuinely laid out as playgrounds (the Meeuwenplaat playground, the schoolyard, and the building playground) have no relationship whatsoever with their surroundings and have been designed in a stony and dreary style.

HOOGVLIET

Analysis of play space in Meeuwenplaat. Physical features (orange = hard landscaped, green = green, black dashed = traffic-free streets) and play facilities (pink labels)

Context and quality

Analysis of the playing potential of both neighbour-hoods leads to a number of observations. First of all, sufficient playing area does not mean by definition that the playing potential is high. In Oude Westen there are many worn-out playing objects. The monotonous structures and stony allure of many play areas limits imaginative and varied possibilities for play. The Meeuwenplaat lacks the seclusion that a good play area needs. Many of the play areas in the Meeuwenplaat are too large-scale for the youngest children. The play objects are so isolated in the wide space that they tend to repel rather than attract. These observations lead to a critical attitude with respect to quantitative norms, such as the 3% norm to which political attention is currently oriented. Sufficient space is the basis for good playing potential, but if the layout does not shape the need for play, even the largest play area fails.

Second, certain age groups have simply been forgotten in both neighbourhoods. Particularly adolescents, adults and the elderly have to do without play opportunities. In Oude Westen, this has resulted in the use of the same locations by various groups (displacement), and in the Meeuwenplaat, young people have simply disappeared from the streetscape. In general, play areas are designed for specific age groups, with the intention to give each group its own niche. It is doubtful whether or not this pre-programmed design of play areas has produced the desired effect. Instead of meeting places, the play areas have become social islands in the neighbourhood due to the sprawl of specific groups. If there is too little space for everyone, age-specific design leads to exclusion. Another disadvantage of age-specific design is that play areas do not fit with the life-cycle of a neighbourhood. If a large group of children remain living in the neighbourhood, the play areas eventually no longer meet the requirements of developing children.

Third, the context turns out to have a great influence on the playing potential. In both neighbourhoods we see the same coloured swings, see-saws, chutes, and racks. The fact that the play typologies for the neighbourhoods differ from one another is a direct consequence of the environment in which the objects have been situated. This determines their user and experiential value. The social structure also has an influence upon the quality requirements of the play area. In contrast to the Meeuwenplaat, the children in Oude Westen almost never have their own garden. This entails that they will make much more intensive use of the public space than the children in the Meeuwenplaat. In the Meeuwenplaat, the play area must primarily have a meeting function to promote the community feeling, whereas in Oude Westen, more attention should be paid to stimulating the individual child's play.

TESTING
PIP

PARTICIPATION

The switch from top-down (directed by government and designers) to a bottom-up (driven by the citizens themselves) development is an essential quality of the historical example that Lefaivre studied. With regard to the playgrounds created by Van Eyck, Mulder and Van Eesteren, this participation was expressed in the correspondence between the residents of the city and the Municipality of Amsterdam. Playgrounds were only constructed when the residents themselves had indicated that they needed them. The idea of a participatory approach is still valid, although the approach is now different. In post-war Amsterdam, citizens' initiatives were followed up by movements within the bureaucratic machine. A present-day form of participation consists of an inspiring co-operation between the designer and the users. In our study, the aim of the participation is primarily to obtain a picture of the local playing culture as a basis for the design of a play network that harmonizes with the play requirement and thus acquires its own allure. For this purpose, children in both neighbourhoods gave us a guided tour of the neighbourhood and made a pictorial report of how and where they play.

In Oude Westen, a group of 20 children from an extra-mural facility, aged from 5 to 13 years, were involved. To prepare the walk-around, these children made drawings of the route they take from school to their homes and of what they encounter on the way. In the Meeuwenplaat, we walked around the neighbourhood in the company of 8 children aged from 5 to 12 years from De Tuimelaar primary school. In addition, a group of youngsters, aged 16 years, gave an independent pictorial report of their vision of playing in the Meeuwenplaat.

To obtain a broad picture of the play culture, we deliberately did not go to the playgrounds, but allowed ourselves to be led by the children to the places that they associate with play. We also asked them to make photos of other things in the neighbourhood on which they had either a positive or negative opinion. Each child was allocated his or her own camera. This turned out to be a play object in itself. The camera and the limited number of photos that they could take with it – 'how many photos do I have left, Miss?' – helped the children to become aware of their environment. Afterwards, we returned with the photos to the children for further information. The photos and the corresponding stories offer a surprising perspective of the experiential world of the child and the role of the play area in it.

OUDE WESTEN

When we went on the excursion with the children in Oude Westen, it was directly obvious that the children dominate the street. They regard almost everywhere as a play area. They are extremely creative in finding something to play with on every stoop, corner and passageway. Columns become goalposts and walls are hiding places or an obstacle course. The coloured posts on one of the inner courts, whose function we did not grasp at first, turned out to be posts for practising their taekwondo kicks.

It was soon evident just how streetwise the children actually are. They move self-confidently through the neighbourhood and, with remarks such as 'Berkel and Roodenrijs, isn't that a farmers' village?' about our place of residence, and 'Look Miss, a junkie' they make it clear that they know exactly what is going on in the world. Besides playing football and using the play equipment, they engage in rapping, breakdance, and generally hanging around. Even the youngest children are independent, almost without exception. They are aware of the danger on the streets and avoid junkies and vagrants. Safety and neatness are recurring topics. Accordingly, the inner courts are the favourite play areas, especially for the younger children. 'It's nice that you can play here in safety.' They children avoid places with dog's dirt and dirty chutes. During the guided tour, we discover that various generations and branches of the same family all live in Oude Westen. The children run into uncles and aunts, they show us where grandma and granddad live, and visit their parents who work in various shops in the district. We regard these social networks as one of the reasons why the children play so independently on the streets. The District Park and the Odeon community centre are places of special significance. Without exception, all the children want to go to the District Park, both the boys and the girls. Here they lie in the grass, have fun – 'Sometimes we throw stones, see who can throw the furthest' – and the children's farm is enormously popular despite its modest dimensions. The fact that gnomes live in the park (according to the children – 'isn't that right Furry?') we initially regarded as the manifestation of a lively imagination. Later we discovered that construction workers lay out gnome paths every year. Because the District Park lies in a rather eccentric situation, most children only play here in the weekend and under supervision. The Odeon is the community centre of Oude Westen and functions as the central meeting place. The children meet many of their friends here. In the covered play area, people can engage in sports outside school hours and numerous activities are organized for residents of Oude Westen. The children photographed many exceptional things, from graffiti and wall art to a flower stall and a toy pistol. Eye-catching

99

100

Snapshots of their play world by children from Oude Westen

cars were popular with both boys and girls. We recognize the same fascination with cars among the adults, too. They make a game of washing their cars. In the photos, clothes and behaviour of the children is becomes obvious that material matters play an important role in the experiential world of the children. The shops and the Kentucky Fried Chicken on the busy traffic streets are an integral part of the play areas of Oude Westen. This becomes clear during the guided tour when a group of boys aged around 10 years spontaneously enter a hifi shop and begin to take photographs. 'We were told to take photos of the places where we play, weren't we!?'

The influence of the city is ubiquitous in the play culture of Oude Westen, as is shown by the fascination for expensive cars, graffiti, rapping, and breakdancing. The independence and judgment of the children are typical urban qualities. The children have a remarkably strong association with places. Even six-year-olds can indicate their houses on the map and know all the street names in the neighbourhood by heart. During the guided tour, they know exactly which places they want to go to and why. Each place evokes a new form of play and its own distinct story. 'Look, that's where I found a bowling ball, there in that corner. And then I threw it down the drain.' The girls of 12 years old only wanted to rap at a 'cool' place with graffiti, thus demonstrating the strong relationship between the game and the place. The urban dynamics is translated directly into play behaviour.

HOOGVLIET

The guided tour of the Meeuwenplaat began rather hesitatingly. Due to the cold weather, not all the children are interested in going out. They find it difficult to show us around with the rather loose assignment to show us where they play. Instead of regarding the large expanses of green as their playground, the children show us the places around the school that have been laid out as play areas. Particularly the (now demolished) playground is popular. What we see as a poorly main-tained collection of anonymous play objects, they regard as a safe playground and a central meeting place in the thinly populated neighbourhood. Almost exclusively, the children of the Meeuwenplaat only play under the supervision of their parents or older brothers. 'I always go with Mum or Dad, because it is quite far. If I go to play somewhere else during the day, some-body takes me there.' Despite the child-friendly structure of the neighbourhood, they do not feel really safe in the neighbourhood, especially due to the cars. The children made a striking number of photos of buildings. These are the houses where they live and of the friends with whom they play. Their stories indicate that they play inside quite a lot. 'I don't have a garden but that doesn't bother me. Because I've got a television and I can watch that,' says Sham, five years old. The girls in particular seldom go to the play area to meet other children at random, but instead they agree to meet to play indoors or in one of the (private) gardens. During the walk-around, we had the impression that the buildings often form an orientation point in the neighbourhood, more than the public space does. The children of the Meeuwenplaat are not really critical of the playing possibilities; they seem to accept everything as it is. The locations where they like to play have more to do with the fact that friends or family live there. The photos display remarkably many natural elements in the surroundings, such as trees, flowers, ducks, dogs, and a cat. This means that the children do acknowledge the green around them. The fact that they primarily play at places that have been laid out, although paved and stony, is thus even more remarkable.

We have the impression that the world of play of the children in the Meeuwenplaat is scarcely nourished by the physical environment. On the contrary: their play behaviour reflects the monotonously laid-out outdoor space. The play culture we observe is characterized by the regulated context within which play occurs, such as within school, in activities arranged by the extra-mural organization, and within the private environment of the home. This play behaviour stands in sharp contrast with the many pictures that the children take of nature – trees, dogs, ducks, flowers. They see the green, but they can't do anything with it.

The children scarcely associate playing with physical space. There are few places that have special significance for them, and they cannot orient themselves well in the neighbourhood. When we ask them to give information on the photos they have taken, they speak in general terms rather than actually dealing with what is shown on the picture. The photos do indicate that the children do pay attention to details. On the other hand, there are many pictures of large open spaces in which play objects seem to stand forlorn in a rather desolate ambience. This gives rise to the idea that the scale of the Meeuwenplaat is too large for the experiential world of the child.

Adolescents in the Meeuwenplaat

Youngsters are very critical about their neighbourhood. They mostly take photos of old rundown buildings, dangerous holes in the road, and muddy (football) fields. They are also conscious of the changes in the neighbourhood. 'They're busy building new houses. Meeuwenplaat will take on a renewed and better appearance. It will no longer been seen as a deprived neighbourhood.' They all find that there are few play areas for their age group. 'The smaller children have been taken into account, but there's no playground for the older kids. They get bored, and that has its consequences.' The limited basketball courts and football fields are poorly maintained and it is even forbidden to play at some places. They feel unwelcome 103 in the neighbourhood. The youngsters mostly feel the need for better football fields and basketball courts and places to chill out. The places that are meant for young people, such as the disco and Flamingo dance school, don't appeal to them. 'That's a kind of clubhouse. All kinds of parties and discos are held there. But they're silly.' Each group has its own place in the Meeuwen-plaat, preferably places they have taken over themselves. An informal hang-out is a good example. This place has been demarcated by the kids by writing and painting on the surrounding trespa panels. Despite the abundance of green, there is always competition for space in the Meeuwenplaat. There are too few places for young people, who are literally barred from some places. The scarce place is the subject of mutual rivalry: each group claims its own area. Just like the clothes they wear and the music they listen to, the places where the young people hang out determine their image. The core of the play culture of adolescents consists of demanding space by transforming a place into an own domain, somewhere they can identify with. The best locations are semi-informal places with benches and shelter, where there is scope to make your own mark.

Snapshots of their play world by children and youngsters from Meeuwenplaat

Local play culture

The guided tours, photos, and discussions with the children have led to a number of conclusions concerning the play culture. In some aspects, this applies to all the children, but there turn out to be local differences too.

What is most noticeable is that the world of play of all children is substantially larger than the playground. Only one fifth of all photos were of furnished play areas. The vast majority show empty spaces, friends, flowers, animals, buildings, and artworks. What the children of both neighbourhoods share is that they are all sensitive to neatness and safety. They prefer not to play at a dirty, poorly maintained, or unsafe place. To a child, the playing potential of a neighbourhood is not only related to the presence of good playgrounds. The general perception of the neighbourhood assumes a more important place in the world of play than was generally thought. A third shared feature that we discovered was that the self-creation of play areas occupies a prominent place in the play culture of all children.

There are particularly striking differences between the play cultures of the neighbourhoods. One often speaks of *the* play behaviour of five to eighteen-year-olds. However, the results of this study qualify this picture. The play behaviour of children of around the same age and background is partly determined by the context. In addition, we recognize a relationship between the urban dynamics and the presence of many small spots in Oude Westen, and the associative and informal play behaviour that the children in that neighbourhood display. The formal play behaviour of the children in the Meeuwenplaat (who mainly play under supervision at the furnished playgrounds) can be explained by the lack of well-defined spots or other points of orientation in the expansive green area. A static environment leads to passive play behaviour. The low child-density in the Meeuwenplaat is another possible cause of the children's need to play at arranged places. A spontaneous meeting with friends simply doesn't happen.

105

TESTING
PIP

INTERSTITIAL

The way in which the playgrounds designed by Aldo van Eyck are situated at residual locations in the urban fabric is defined by Lefaivre as 'interstitial'. Their distinctive quality lies in the way in which they harmonize with the urban fabric. A natural opening in the urban structure is transformed into a play area. In the post-war Amsterdam city centre, these interstitial places consisted of spaces that arose as the result of demolition, or were available at intersections. In the urban expansion district of the Westelijke Tuinsteden (West Garden Cities) in Amsterdam, these were the communal inner courts. Every courtyard was assigned its own playground, where the youngest children could play safely under the watchful eye of their parents. Besides their spatial quality, these places also have an exceptional social quality: a natural embedding of play areas within sight of the houses has a positive effect upon the accessibility and the use of the play facility, and ensures a measure of social control.

In terms of spatial structure, Oude Westen is similar to the inner city of Amsterdam, and the patterned structure of the Meeuwenplaat resembles the Westelijke Tuinsteden. In both neighbourhoods, investigation was carried out to identify the interstitial spaces in the urban fabric and the relationship between these places and their use as play areas.

OUDE WESTEN

In the fine-meshed structure of Oude Westen, almost all the public space is interstitial space. Most squares were created by the demolition of parts of building blocks, and are thus well entrenched in the urban fabric. At most squares, direct supervision is possible from the surrounding houses and this provides sufficient social control for safe children's play.

The stoops are another kind of interstitial space. These places were deliberately designed with set-back street alignment to create space in the narrow streets. These small bays border on the fronts of the houses and form a transitional zone between the front door and public space. They are mainly furnished with one or two play objects. Due to their position, size and layout, they are primarily suited to the youngest children.

The urban unit of Oude Westen is the closed block. As a consequence, the (semi-)public inner courts are an integral part of the architectural structure and they form extraordinary interstitial locations. By giving them a layout as communal places and by making them partly or wholly public, they have acquired an exceptional function. Physically screened off from the street, they form a transitional zone between the house and the street, or an extension to the house.

Space is scarce in Oude Westen and there is a great need for more play area. Accordingly, it is unfortunate that there are many interstitial spaces in Oude Westen that do not, or hardly, offer any opportunities for play. The lateral connections are a conspicuous example of   107 lost opportunity. These car-free streets are an exception to the north-south pattern of traffic veins, and thus form informal routes in the urban fabric. With this, they assume an exceptional quality as potential play areas. One disadvantage is the fact that social supervision is lacking because the lateral connections are often surrounded by blank walls.

Safety is an important theme in Oude Westen and these interstitial places would be ideal in providing just that. To children, it is of great importance that they have the feeling that they are not shut in, and that they always have an overview of the space around them. The interstitial spaces that are too dark and/or are only open on one side are therefore not suitable as play areas.

HOOGVLIET

In the expansive set-up of the post-war neighbourhood of the Westelijke Tuinsteden in Amsterdam, the communal inner courts work as closed, interstitial play areas. At first sight, the inner courts of the Meeuwenplaat also seem to meet the spatial criteria. Play objects have been situated in a number of inner courts. However, children make almost no use of these facilities. The explanation of the limited user quality lies in a subtle yet crucial difference with the inner courts of the Westelijke Tuinsteden. In contrast to this Amsterdam patterned neighbourhood, where the houses border directly on the green, there is no relationship whatsoever between the houses and the green areas in the Meeuwenplaat. Storage areas are situated on the ground floor of the gallery and porch flats that adjoin the courts. The communal entrances are oriented toward the street. There is no direct access from the houses to the green courts. The residents have to walk along their street and around the block to make use of the green area. The poor relationship between the courts and the houses reduces the play potential of the courts, which consequently become passive visual green strips.

In contrast, children and adults tend to gather at the corners and entrances of the blocks. These are the lively places that have a direct relationship with the houses and where there is some form of supervision. To adults, too, the corners of the blocks are the play areas where they lay out small street-front gardens. In the central zone, where the single-family homes have been built, the garden paths can be regarded as interstitial space. Because these are free of motorized traffic and directly adjoin the houses, they are safe places for young children. These paths have not been laid out as play areas, but they do form natural secluded play places. The expressive street-front gardens and hedges can be regarded as informal play areas for adults.

The corners, the entrance zones and the garden paths mark the interstitial space, which is just as surprising as it is self-evident, of the Meeuwenplaat.

The power of the in-between

Interstitial places can assume various spatial shapes. A residual spot, an extra broad stoop, an inner court, a corner between two blocks, they are all in-between places. Nevertheless, not every interstitial space is a good place to play. What the good places have in common is that they mark the transition between public and private areas. They are places that are close to the front door and within view of the houses. These are particularly important places for young children, because they can play there safely yet independently. To adults, they are places where they can spontaneously put down a bench or a flowerpot, and can open a conversation with the neighbours. Young people can see and be seen in optimum fashion. People always manage to find these places intuitively. Just as with an animal track, these places can be traced in every neighbourhood by watching where the users go. The play potential can be articulated by adding elements or by creating small niches where the residents themselves are challenged to add something to the public space. Much attention is devoted to the safety of play objects. The European norms for safety that have been recorded in the Attraction Act are constantly being stiffened. A child may no longer run the risk of a scratch or bruise. The regulations covering the play area itself are conspicuous by their absence with regard to the *choice* of location. Based on the location of the available space and often in an attempt to restrict nuisance, play areas are often situated at invisible spots on the edges of the neighbourhood – a policy that leads to socially insecure situations. The spatial and social quality of the in-between spaces make the concept of 'interstitial' an applicable one for identifying places that are suitable for transformation into play areas.

109

TESTING PIP

POLYCENTRIC

In the PIP model, the term 'polycentric' refers to the density of the play network. The building blocks of the network are the interstitial spaces that were gradually transformed, bottom-up, into play areas in post-war Amsterdam. These play areas were all different, but bore the same recognizable signature of Aldo van Eyck. After the analysis of the play culture (Participation) and the spatial qualities of the neighbourhood (Interstitial), the term 'polycentric' in our practical study has been given significance in a design proposal for a network of play areas for the Oude Westen and the Meeuwenplaat. This network is spread like extended tissue across the neighbourhoods. The merit of the tissue is its high density. The small places are stepping stones from which the youngest children, step by step, can discover the public space around them.

The proposal for the play network gives a present-day interpretation to the historical example. In the post-war period, attention was mainly devoted to play areas for younger children. Now there are also other age groups that are under pressure in public urban space, such as adolescents and senior citizens. Accordingly, the modern variant of the play network offers playing space for people of all ages.

In addition, Van Eyck's playgrounds were relatively universal in their set-up. The function of the play network was unilaterally oriented toward children's play. The layout of the playgrounds in the inner city of Amsterdam did not really differ from that in the Weste-lijke Tuinsteden. In our proposals, the play network responds to its specific context by reflecting and re-inforcing the local character. In this way, a play network that enhances the liveability of the neigh-bourhood and assigns identity to the public space is generated.

OUDE WESTEN

The play network in Oude Westen reflects the play culture there by giving form and scope to informal and varying play behaviour. This is achieved by creating a landscape-oriented layout with many subtle possibilities for play. The play network strengthens the spatial qualities by bringing organized diversity to the monotonous stony design of the current play areas. The intention is to improve the spatial experience in the tight urban structure. Finally, the play network provides, to a greater extent than the current public space, meeting places for people of different ages and backgrounds. It offers an infrastructure for the social coherence that is currently so conspicuously absent in the neighbourhood. The various functions of the network are give form in three layers.

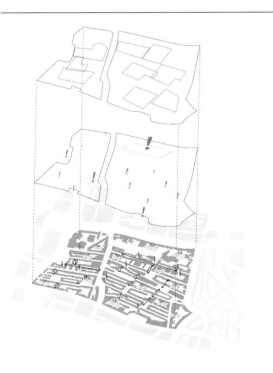

Three-dimensional play network for Oude Westen: interstitial layer (bottom), theme layer (middle), connecting layer (top).

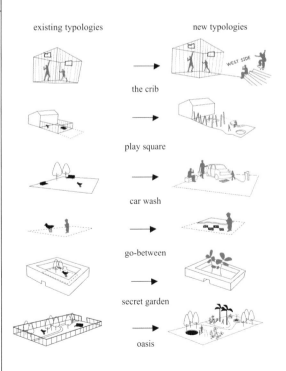

Substantiation of the play network, which reinforces the existing typologies.

The interstitial layer: (top) the Go-between, informal play space; (top right) the Instant Playground, temporary play space; (bottom right) the Secret Garden, transformation of the inner courts.

References: informal card game for the elderly in Shanghai, water fountain as a landscape play element, mobile merry-go-round in Istanbul and a playground, Barcelona.

Interstitial layer

The in-between places – the inner courts, the lateral streets, and the other residual places, are the spatial bearers of this layer. The play areas in this layer mainly satisfy the needs of small children and senior citizens who want or have to stay close to home. The layout of the areas tends to be informal. By making use of similar colours, materials and forms at all the places, a recognizable network is created in a subtle manner. The play areas are deliberately not substantiated with pre-programmed playing equipment. Instead, the emphasis is placed on multifunctional, landscape elements. These play areas, which ought to last the lifespan of a child (thus suitable for all ages), are less sensitive to wear and tear than the vulnerable equipment. Not all the interstitial spaces are furnished with objects. This allows scope for personal sub-stantiation, varying from a children's bath or pool to a barbecue or table on which people can play chess. Other forms of temporary substantiation are artworks and manifestations. The dimensions of the lateral streets make them particularly suited to this purpose.

The inner courts are semi-public spaces that are designed as secret green gardens with labyrinths, covered sitting places, and a holiday village for the gnomes who, according to the children, live in the District Park. These inner gardens can be filled in by the residents according to their own requirements and enriched with other elements. In this way, an interaction game for young and old is created.

Theme layer

In contrast to the interstitial layer, the play areas in the theme layer are designed to be distinctive from one another. This layer consists of larger squares measuring around 600 m^2. The individual character of the places is reinforced by designing them with themes that are derived from the existing play culture and other characteristic elements of Oude Westen. This could be a 'bling' hang-out for adolescents, based on present-day pop culture or a tough West Side – a local nickname for Oude Westen – sports enclosure with its own place for graffiti. The places that allow this, in terms of size, such as the District Park, are laid out in such a way that they bring various age groups together, the *intergenerational* places. The play areas are not designed around the age group but rather around the lifestyle. One example is the *Car Wash* site, where adults convene to wash their cars while the youth can talk about the cars and the youngest children can play with self-made constructions of rubber tyres.

The thematic approach entrenches variety and surprise in the urban fabric. A perception of spatiality is created by having the layout of the places contrast with their

surroundings in terms of material and colour, and linking them together in terms of visual and spatial properties.

The variety of images gives a backdrop effect that reinforces the spatiality of the neighbourhood.

The connecting layer

The connecting layer establishes a functional, physical and visual link between the separate places. It is the cement of the network. The point of departure is the creation of small traffic-free routes – walk-arounds – between the various spots. Places and routes form one continuum. Particularly the lateral connections have a double function and are place and route at the same time. It is not a choice between playing or walking around, but rather a matter of moving from place to place while playing, exactly as the children in Oude Westen currently do. The deliberate design reinforces the play culture already present. The routes are allocated a sporting function as obstacle courses or skating itineraries. The link between the users and the physical space is assigned special attention in this layer by means of (inter)active play events in which children can mark a certain route (temporarily) using drawing chalk, paint or spray cans.

114

The theme layer: (top) the Car Wash, referring to the local play culture of car washing (bottom) the Crib, referring to the urban play behaviour of children in Oude Westen.

References: play furniture made of used tyres by 2012 architects, sports area on Venice Beach, Los Angeles.

The binding layer:
the Play Path, sporting route for young and old.

Reference: play area in Warsaw.

HOOGVLIET

The play network in the Meeuwenplaat has to ensure that the natural need to play, both in children and in adults, is physically better supported that is currently the case. This is achieved by, among other things, strengthening the distinction between space and place in the neighbourhood, situating play areas at the corners that are now being used informally, and by creating recognizable domains for various groups. Play areas again become meeting places and locations to which people feel attached.

The qualities present in the Meeuwenplaat, in the form of abundant greenery, are accentuated by giving the green a more varied and active role. The network enters a relationship with its environment by referring to the local flora and the rich history of the fishing village that became a post-war neighbourhood and then a new-construction suburb. The play area supports the social-cultural structure present in the neighbourhood by giving each independently-functioning quarter a play network with its own identity and function. These interventions are structures in a network with three different layers.

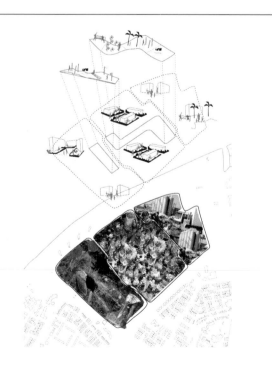

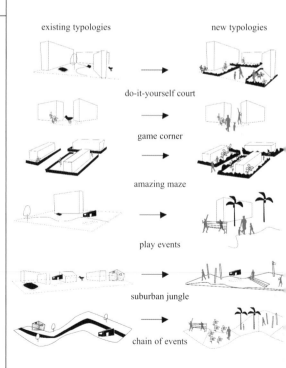

existing typologies　　　new typologies

do-it-yourself court

game corner

amazing maze

play events

suburban jungle

chain of events

Three-dimensional play network for Meeuwenplaat: theme layer (bottom), interstitial layer (middle), connecting layer (top).

Substantiation of the play network, which reinforces the existing typologies.

Theme layer

The theme layer is a basis that reinforces the characters of the various zones in the Meeuwenplaat. Each quarter is allocated a guiding design theme for the layout of the play area. This theme gives form to the spatial and social features present. Giving the locations a theme improves the orientation. The zoning also has a social effect.

By reinforcing the character of each quarter, the residents are more able to identify with their neighbourhood and make the space their own. In this way, the connection between the residents and the outdoor space, and among the residents themselves, is reinforced at local level.

The north zone is allocated the idea of the *building place* as the guiding design theme. This quarter, in particular, will be a huge building site in the coming years. The building site can thus emphasize the dynamic character of the quarter. The accent will be put on industrial, urban building-place play locations. The foundations of the buildings will be a play area in themselves. Recollections of intensive restructuring will be immortalized in play locations made of demolition material.

The central zone will be laid out according to the metaphor of the *gnome village*. With the many gardens featuring artistically trimmed hedges and personally laid-out gardens with garden gnomes, windmills and statues, the quarter already has a small-scale character. This is reinforced by giving the limited public space an intimate allure by adding flower beds and artworks that have been inspired by the playfulness of garden ornaments.

The south zone will have *garden allotment* as its theme. The emphasis will lie on strengthening a sense of community by creating real meeting places.

The characteristic courts that are little used at present can be transformed into play landscapes, for example, with semi-private gardens and vegetable gardens.

Interstitial layer

The building blocks of this layer are the in-between places of the Meeuwenplaat, because they mark the transition zones between the private sphere of the home and the public sphere of the street: the edges and corners of blocks, the intervening paths and, to a lesser degree, the inner courts. To an important extent, this layer provides do-it-yourself places that challenge one to demonstrate creative play behaviour. They meet the need of various age groups to make the anonymous green area their own. The places are laid out according to the principle of comprehensive playing potential. Instead of installing formal playing equipment from the catalogues, the emphasis lies on the addition of more landscape elements such as lines on the street, the use of miscellaneous materials, walls, ledges, and ambiguous objects. The corners in particular will be allocated sitting facilities, preferably in the form of elements that also have another (playing) function besides that of a seat.

The residents will be actively involved in the set-up of this layer, via manifestations, neighbourhood festivities and design competitions, for example. Designing a public space becomes a game that brings the residents closer together. The layout of the individual places will be linked to the overarching theme for the quarter. For the north zone, one could think of a graffiti wall or climbing face. A (temporary) youth centre could be set up in one of the vacant buildings, where youngsters under the supervision of designers of artists, for example, could be responsible for the design, reconstruction and operation of the project. In this way, this forgotten age group finally receives its own place thanks to the restructuring scheme.

A garden competition could be held in the central zone: who is the best hedge-trimmer, or cultivates the most exceptional garden? Accordingly, the individual passion for gardening brings a positive impulse to the (semi-) public space and connects people with their surroundings and with one another.

In the south zone, the residents can manipulate the corners and entrance areas by laying out street-front greenery and making sitting or hang-out sites. An architectural intervention allowing the apartment blocks to directly access the inner courts generates the possibility of converting the currently monotonous structures into playing or gardening areas. In an ideal situation, the inner courts – in co-operation with the schools in the vicinity, for example – could bring the various generations together by having the elder people teach the younger ones how to look after a garden.

Connecting layer

The connecting layer is directed at combining the spatial and social structures in the Meeuwenplaat. By creating special places at the transitions of the various quarters and allowing these places to contrast strongly with their surroundings in terms of design, the quarters are physically and visually linked together. The play zones are laid out with play equipment for various age categories. These zones are more formal in their nature than those in other layers of the network. They are central meeting places between the various generations, and each group has its own domain. The locations that lend themselves *par excellence* for this function are the green swathe and the school strip. The natural character of the Meeuwenplaat is reinforced in the green swathe. In this zone, one can install an adventure playground

The theme layer: The Building Site, referring to the intensive restructuring in this zone.

Reference: Bauspielplatz ('Building-play space') in Hamburg. In Germany, the Bauspielplatz is a frequently-occurring feature that is also found in inner-city areas.

The interstitial layer: (bottom left) The Amazing Maze, imaginative play space in the narrow streets of the central zone; (bottom right) Games Corner and Hangout Corner, temporary play spaces for young and old with mobile play furnishings.

References: play equipment for the elderly in Shanghai, chess square in Rotterdam, Crate by Guido Marsille, 2006.

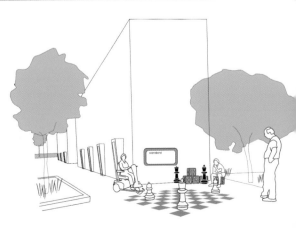

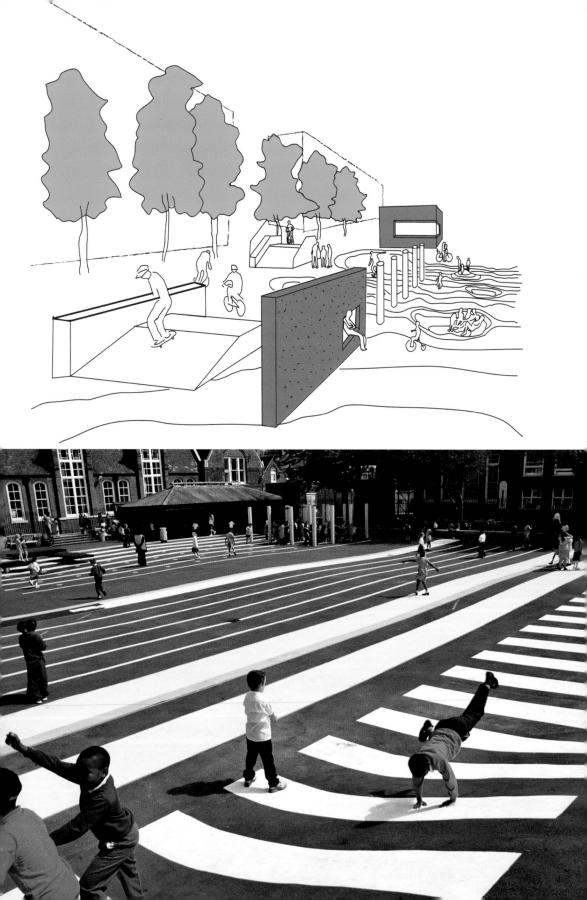

The connecting layer: (top) The Chain of Events, reinforcement of the existing green swathe to a natural play domain; (left) The Suburban Jungle, the play space in the school strip is assigned an urban allure.

References: Playground in Switzerland, Experimental Playground, London, by Snug and Outdoor, 2003.

with tree huts, a fishing pond, a children's farm, and a garden for plucking summer flowers. By basing the plant assortment on the original flora of the Meeuwenplaat, a morphological reference to the natural origins of the neighbourhood will arise. The existing 'parasite', a temporary building, can be converted into a specific nature education centre. These interventions give a positive impulse to the image of the entire neighbourhood. The school strip will become a play strip which, in contrast to the green swathe, has a more stony structure and an emphasis on play and sports.

One model, two networks

Depending on the social, spatial and cultural context, the same starting points for the play network produce two different models for a play network. The network in Oude Westen has the goal of reinforcing the spatial feeling by applying contrasts in the design of the squares, while zoning in the Meeuwenplaat reduces the monotonous space to a scale that harmonizes with the quarter-oriented social structure. In the fine-meshed structure of Oude Westen, the interstitial places in the urban fabric are the bearers of the network. By mutually connecting many relatively small places, a classic polycentric network is created, as in the inner city of Amsterdam after the war. The scale of the Meeuwenplaat is too large to create the same kind of network. The small playgrounds would be lost in space. The scale of the building blocks of the network must correspond to the scale of the space and the intensity of usage. A certain user-density is needed in order to realize a lively playground. For the Meeuwenplaat, this means fewer but larger places where various groups can convene without getting in one another's way.

Because the inner courts of the Meeuwenplaat do not have a physical relationship with the houses, a small playground will not be installed on every inner court, in contrast to the historical example of the Westelijke Tuinsteden in Amsterdam. The extent to which there is a genuine polycentric network remains debatable and is probably a question of definition. Whatever the case, a fine-meshed urban fabric lends itself better for a network of small playgrounds than an expansive set-up. One correspondence between the models is that they both consist of several layers. To give the various groups their own place and also ensure that a connection is created, the network is not only polycentric but also three-dimensional. Each layer has its own function. Collectively, the places form a network due to the fact that they are interconnected via physical routes, sightlines, or meeting zones.

121

DESIGN STRATEGY FOR PLAY NETWORKS

Reflection

The basis of the study was the observation that play areas are scarcely seen as issues of architectonic design. They are also often situated at unattractive and even unsafe locations on the edge of a neighbourhood. They are isolated from the urban structure. The playground has a special function in public space. Play brings people together. In the light of the current discussion on liveability and the place of the child in the city, play areas can provide a solution. This will not happen as long as the reference remains the playground in the catalogue. To realize their true potential, a new perspective on play in the city is needed. This book presents a vision on play in the city. It is a vision in which form and space give scope to *homo ludens*, and play areas give identity to the environment.

Liane Lefaivre developed the PIP model for the urban design of playgrounds. This model is based on the historical example of the post-war playgrounds that were created by means of a co-operative effort between Aldo van Eyck, Cor van Eesteren and Jacoba Mulder. PIP stands for Participation, Interstitial (the in-between), and Polycentric. Participation refers to the interactive processes between the residents and the Municipality in which the playgrounds were realized. The playgrounds only arose when the residents informed the local authorities that they needed them. Another merit of the playgrounds lies in the extent to which they fit into the urban fabric, a factor designated by Lefaivre by the term 'interstitiality'. The natural embedding of the playgrounds ensures better user quality and promotes social control. Collectively, these playgrounds form a polycentric network, a tissue with a high density of small playing areas.

Architect's office *Döll – Atelier voor Bouwkunst* investigated the PIP model as a present-day architectural design strategy for a network of play areas for all ages that assigns identity to public space. The test locations were two Rotterdam neighbourhoods currently undergoing a restructuring process: the inner-city Oude Westen and the post-war Meeuwenplaat in Hoogvliet. Reflection on the PIP model study leads to a practice-oriented scenario for a play network.

Design strategy for play networks

The design strategy establishes a scenario for a gradual and sustainable development of a play network. The PIP model is the basis of the scenario. There are two important supplementary starting points for the design studies. The first is that the play network must offer play potential to all age groups. The second point is that the play network must enter into a relationship with its environment. The design of the play spaces gives form to the specific local elements, including the play culture. These starting points are interwoven in the PIP model. In this way, a design strategy for a scenario for a play network is created, consisting of three elements: participation, structure and identity.

Participation
The first step in the design strategy is a participatory approach. A good play network is not designed on the drawing table. Participation reinforces the involvement and latent support of the residents and leads to greater user appreciation of the play area realized. Participation also furnishes insight into the local play culture. The spatial translation of the children's style of play, fascinations, and experience of the neighbourhood leads to a meaningful play area with high user quality. During the study phase, the play culture is made visible by means of a photographic project in which children give a guided tour of the neighbourhood and, in doing so, create a pictorial report of all facets of their play world. The design stage has participatory elements in the form of a design competition, the joint creation of scale models or mood boards with reference images. The starting point is the collective determination of the basis concept or the ambience, not the entrustment of the design. A strict supervision of the design process is a precondition of a good result.

As a component of the actual realization, the children help to realize the play areas. The realization of play space becomes a playful process that, in itself, brings people together. The play areas may have a temporary character by the addition of mobile elements, or the painting of stoops and streets. Thus, the children themselves determine the places where they want to play. The temporary play areas form the basis of a permanent design. The involvement of residents in the management stage is most effective when organized co-operation between the local authorities and the residents brings benefits to everyone. This may involve joint management as a component of the activities and educational programme of local institutions such as the schools or community centres.

Structure
The second element in the design strategy is the formulation of the spatial structure of the play network. The play network consists of three design principles: interstitial, polycentric, and three-dimensional.
Interstitial: the in-between places are the building blocks of the structure. They are light, open spaces that fit seamlessly in the urban structure, and are nestled at the transitions between public and private areas. Due to their visual and physical relationship with the adjoining houses in terms of supervision and access, they are primarily suitable for the youngest children. The places

most attractive to adults are those that they can appropriate by creating street-front gardens and placing garden furniture.
Polycentric: the in-between places are gradually transformed into a fine-meshed network of small niches in the neighbourhood. Their merit lies in the high density. The places form stepping stones via which the child can discover the neighbourhood step by step in a playful manner. Playing becomes an integral part of the experience of the neighbourhood. This certainly does not mean that the entire neighbourhood is filled with playing equipment. The small play spaces in particular are laid out to harmonize with the landscape. In this context, one can consider the placement of low walls to sit on, to jump over, or to hide behind, the application of subtle differentiation in the ground structure, and the artistic deployment of lighting, colour and water that have been designed with play in mind.
Three-dimensional: To allow scope for various play functions, the network consists of several layers. A fine-meshed play network, embedded in the landscape, offers space for informal (children's) games. A second layer provides larger places that are set up around a certain lifestyle or play style. Accordingly, people of different ages and background are brought together. These layers are connected visually and functionally, via play routes from place to place or a course for skating or jogging. In this way, individual play areas become a play network.

Identity
The play network acquires its own distinct character by entering into a relationship with its surroundings. In conjunction with other place-oriented features in the social, spatial and historical context, the play culture offers inspiration for innovative play concepts with a recognizable allure. Play areas become places to which people feel attached. For example, the passion for washing cars in Oude Westen was translated in the study into a car wash site where adults can meet while their children play together on the playing facilities that they have made themselves with used car tyres.
There are two different architectural approaches to the substantiation of individual places. The one approach is primarily directed to the creation of unity by realizing a recognizable signature in colour, form and material at all the play areas in a quarter, neighbourhood or city. In the spatial experience, this repetition generates a self-evident network.
Another approach is a distinctive substantiation of the play areas. The play area becomes a landmark in the urban fabric. The advantage of an approach that is oriented toward distinction instead of uniformity is that groups then identify more with their own place. This

can also lead to tensions in public order. The layered network interweaves the best of both worlds. A layer of playgrounds that are laid out in more landscape-like manner is combined with a network of play areas set up according to themes that differ strongly from one another. In this way, every function receives its own form and significance. However, not every place that is a component of the play network is designed. The network also offers figurative play areas by including small, free zones that residents can fill temporarily.

The city is a playground
In the present study, the design strategy for a play network is projected on to areas due to be restructured. The design strategy also provides points of contact for an architectural approach to play areas in new-construction suburbs. Play may even be a *leitmotiv* for the architectural design. A thematic substantiation of the places can be found in the historical or natural references of the location. In this case, too, the play network develops gradually and bottom-up. Not all the space is programmed in advance. New residents are involved in the development of their own world of play. A participatory design process brings people closer together and creates the infrastructure for the genesis of a lively play and neighbourhood culture.

The scenario for a play network can also be applied to city centres. The city offers sufficient physical play space to create a network of play areas. The integration of play areas in the centre is one of the great qualities of public space in cities such as Barcelona or Paris, and serves as an example. The skate park on the intermediate strip between the busy traffic artery of Westblaak in Rotterdam demonstrates the positive effect that play can have on the allure of a city. Initially there was much antipathy toward the advent of the skate park but resolve eventually led to success. The skate park gives an extra identity not only this location but also to Rotterdam as a whole. A new lunchroom and various shops that are specialized in skate and board articles have opened here. The combination of a prominent location, an advanced level of ambition, and play repays itself. The entrepreneurs in the Beurstraverse shopping street also benefit from the play potential that was created here with the water jets that leap out of the street grids on sunny days. Children are attracted to them like bears to honey and take their parents to these places to do their shopping.
A play-oriented inner city gives a positive allure and offers genuine opportunities for people from different backgrounds to come together. These examples illustrate the fact that a play network does not have to

124

Process	**Participation as the motor for ground-up development**	
	Study	Charting the children's own world of play by getting them to produce drawings and photos.
	Design	Competition, scale models, etc. by future users as input for the design.
	Implementation	Playscapes: independent manipulation of the outdoor space as play form.
	Management	Collective management forms bring people together.
Structure	**Designing a new layer in the urban fabric**	
	Interstitial	In-between places are the building blocks for a play network.
	Polycentric	The separate playgrounds jointly form a layer in the urban fabric.
	Multidimensional	A network that allows scope to various age groups consists of several layers.
Identity	**Reinforcing local elements in the design of the play spaces**	
	Social	The things that bind and divide people as the starting point for the creation of meeting places: intergenerational and age-specific.
	Spatial	Reacting to the urban blueprint by means of uniformity or diversity of spaces.
	Cultural	Local play culture of children and adults as a source of inspiration.

be neighbourhood-based. The context determines the elaboration but, in every context, the play network offers a tissue of low-threshold public space that creates the urban conditions for meeting and exchanging, and within which play is elevated to urban culture.

Acknowledgments

The authors would like to thank Christopher Alexander, Janneke Arkesteijn, Dimitri Balamotis, Willemien Bosch, Marlies Boterman, Christine Boyer, Hans Beunderman, Margaret Crawford, Karina Daskalov, Teddy Cruz, Aldo and Hannie van Eyck, Dan Graham, David Fischli, Annemieke Fontein, Rudi Fuchs, Adelina von Furstenberg, Arjan Hebly, Cathy Ho, Hans Ulrich Obrist, Elinor Jansz, Richard Ingersoll, Erna Jolles, Claudia Jolles, Rosemarie Maas, Yan Meng, Joan Ockman, Jurgen Rosemann, Jerome Sans, Susan Solomon, Michael Sorkin, David Weiss, Mark Wigley, Erwin Wurm, Ingeborg de Roode, Erik Schmitz, Mariet Schoenmakers, Fritz Schroeder, Mary Otis Stevens, Ernst Strouhal, and Alexander Tzonis for their support at the various stages of this project.

For their participation and photography we would especially like to thank Edward Boele and the children of the WENK foundation (Oude Westen), the students of the Einsteinlyceum (Hoogvliet) and the children of primary school De Tuimelaar (Hoogvliet)

Picture credits

(t = top, m = middle, b = bottom, l = left, r = right)

Andres Ambauen 113t
Carolina Attadil 11t
Ruben Dario 29mr
Alijd van Doorn 14, 15, 18t, 30mr, 32r, 84, 88b, 89b
Henk Döll 9b, 11b, 118l, 121t
Richard van Emmerik 7t
Gemeenterachief Rotterdam 84t
Gosia Grubba 8t, 17b, 18b, 21b, 30ml, 31ml, 31mr, 31r, 32l, 112, 113t, 115, 119
Alex Hartley 29r
Sander Hazevoet 120t
Lisa Jacobs 8b
Erik Jansen 87m, 88m, 89t, 93, 94, 95, 97, 101tr, 107, 109
Kartoview 87t
Greg Keating 7b, 114b
Immo Klink 30l
Rienk Landstra 9t
Olaf Leiter 10, 13, 118t
Suzanne Loen 10t, 12t, 20b
Rick Messemaker 19t, 33l
Momoko Matsumoto 30r
Museum of Contemporary Art, Chicago 19b, 33mr
Eppo Nootenboom 83
Frantisek Staud 32mr
Ingo Vetter 16t, 17t
Uwe Walter 34r
Dada Wang 20t
Blanca Wennekes 12b
Marc Wetli 33r
Joost Woertman 22b
Patrick Wüthrich 21t

127

Credits
The research and this book were both made
possible by the generous support of the Netherlands
Architecture Fund, the Van Eesteren-Fluck & Van
Lohuizen Foundation, Jantje Beton National Youth
Fund, the Art and Public Space Foundation, and the
Faculty of Architecture at Delft University of
Technology.

Research and text
Liane Lefaivre
Döll – Atelier voor Bouwkunst:
Henk Döll and Alijd van Doorn, with the assistance of
Suzanne Loen (drawings), Machteld Berghauser-Pont
and Martijn Jordans

Translation from the
Dutch and English text editing
George Hall

Graphic design
Ben Laloua/Didier Pascal
assisted by Anton Klein

Printed by
Die Keure, Bruges

ISBN 978 90 6450 602 4